Secret Bankside

John Constable is a playwright, poet and performer who has lived for more than twenty years in The Borough. *The Southwark Mysteries*, his epic cycle of poems and mystery plays inspired by the history of the area, was performed in Shakespeare's Globe and Southwark Cathedral. He is also well known for staging site-specific community dramas, notably at Cross Bones Graveyard, and for his unusual historical walks, some of which were created especially for the London Borough of Southwark and for The City of London Festival. A collection of John Constable's *Sha-Manic Plays*, his stage adaptation of Mervyn Peake's *Gormenghast* trilogy and *The Southwark Mysteries* are all available from Oberon Books.

Wenceslaus Hollar, 'Long View of London' (1636–42), detail

Secret Bankside

WALKS IN THE OUTLAW BOROUGH

JOHN CONSTABLE

OBERON BOOKS
LONDON

First published in 2007 by Oberon Books Ltd,
521 Caledonian Road, London N7 9RH
Tel 020 7607 3637 / Fax 020 7607 3629
info@oberonbooks.com / www.oberonbooks.com

A catalogue record for this book is available from the British Library.

Cover design by Oberon Books

Cover photographs by Katie Nicholls
with the exception of the photograph from page 15 by Gary Neale

ISBN 1 84002 743 6 / 978-1-84002-743-3

Printed in Great Britain by Antony Rowe Ltd, Chippenham.

mum

Contents

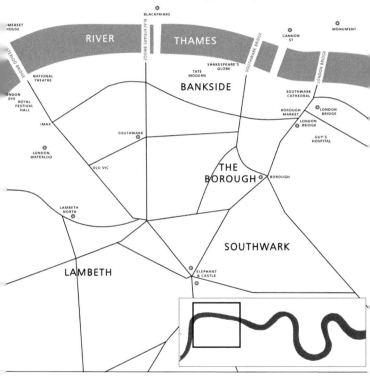

Preamble

Where?

London is, and always has been, two cities: 'north' and 'south of the river' – and nowhere has the divide been deeper than along the stretch of the Thames from Lambeth Bridge to Tower Bridge. The north bank is dominated by Westminster, with the Houses of Parliament, and The City of London, a global financial market. Historically, these ancient seats of political and economic power have looked warily across the river at the wilds of Lambeth and at Southwark, the outlaw borough on the south bank.

This little book of walks explores the most historic – yet, until recently, largely forgotten – part of London, south of the River Thames. Strictly speaking, these are walks around Bankside – that stretch of the south bank between Blackfriars Bridge and London Bridge, just over the river from St Paul's Cathedral and The City of London.

Some of the walks head further west, upstream as far as Waterloo, taking in The South Bank arts complex and the area formerly known as Lambeth Marsh. Some push eastwards, downstream to Tower Bridge. Others venture south, inland, through the back-streets of The Borough, Southwark – the oldest part of London, and at its very heart – now home to one of the most diverse populations in the world.

What?

Each walk explores a different aspect of the area's history and cultural identity.

The Outlaw Borough sets the scene, looking at how the stories of Bankside and the nearby Borough were shaped by their location on the south bank, outside the law of The City of London to the north. It's a tale of prisons – and of 'Liberties', including The Liberty of The Clink, where brothels were licensed by Bishops. In medieval London such activities, whilst forbidden within The City*, were permitted in designated areas outside the city walls or, as on Bankside, south of the river. The Borough was itself a haven for outlaws and prone to periodic outbreaks of Mob rule.

Shakespeare's Bankside develops this theme, evoking the world of Shakespeare and his contemporaries. Theatres came south to Bankside for the same reason the brothels did, because they were forbidden in The City. So it was that Shakespeare's plays came to be written and performed, not in the rarefied atmosphere of a university, still less in provincial Stratford, but in a riotous red-light district.

The Dickens! visits places in The Borough connected with Charles Dickens' life and work – both of which were profoundly influenced by his childhood stay here and by this encounter with London's criminal underclass. In the 19th Century, The Borough had some of the most deprived and lawless slums in London, where even policemen feared to tread.

New Theatre Land begins at The National Theatre, which opened by Waterloo Bridge in 1976. By then, this stretch of the south bank waterfront had effectively been reinvented – as The South Bank† – for the 1951 Festival of Britain. A short walk south of the river, by Waterloo Station, stands the Old Vic, a theatre since 1818. This walk visits both theatres then heads along The Cut, past the Young Vic, into the back-streets further east to take in a world of fringe theatres and site-specific performances.

The Ghost Walk finds magic and mystery on a walk from Elephant and Castle to London Bridge – haunted pubs and music halls; a Borough magician and a female gladiator; the

---

*   The naming of parts of London can be confusing to the uninitiated. When written in lower case, 'the city' is a general reference to the entire metropolis. When capitalised, however, 'The City of London' refers only to the 'Square Mile', that part of the city on the north bank originally surrounded by walls. The boundaries of The City can be deduced from the names of its original gates: Ludgate, Newgate, Aldersgate, Cripplegate, Moorgate, Bishopsgate and Aldgate. For more than a millennium, The City has been an international financial centre.

†   The 'South Bank' (capital letters) refers specifically to the arts complex and environs at Waterloo Bridge – as opposed to the 'south bank' (lower case), which is used more generally to describe the urban waterfront south of the river.

outcast dead of Cross Bones Graveyard, the legend of Mary Overie and the spookiest stretch of the River Thames.

Tate To Elephant takes us from Tate Modern art gallery, an international visitor attraction, to the Elephant and Castle, now in the process of 'regeneration', by way of a short-cut through what was once St George's Fields. Along the way we discover many hidden facets of south London history.

Charlie Chaplin's Memory Lane goes down the Walworth Road and into the back-streets where Chaplin was born and raised. With most common land sacrificed to factories and tenement housing, the Victorian working class resorted to taverns and public pleasure gardens, 'penny gaff' theatres and music halls like the South London Palace of Varieties.

A Healing Pilgrimage takes Chaucer's *Canterbury Tales*, which begin in Southwark, as the starting point for a walk about 'healing' in an urban environment: from Guy's and the original St Thomas' Hospital to the former Bedlam, taking in the sites of old prisons and burial grounds, which have since been reclaimed as public parks and gardens.

How?

Each walk is preceded by a map, with the location of each site visited on the route clearly numbered, as well as a brief overview, giving practical information about its theme, length, and starting and ending points. The principal sites visited on each walk are numbered both in the overview and within the chapter itself, enabling the reader to locate them quickly and easily on the map.

The nearest underground station is also included. The area covered by the walks is relatively small, and they begin and end within walking distance of one or more of these stations: London Bridge, Borough, Elephant and Castle, Lambeth North, Southwark or Waterloo. There are overground railway stations at London Bridge, Elephant and Castle and Waterloo. This part of London is also well served by buses. To avoid overwhelming the reader with information, a specific bus number is only given where there is no rail or underground station within easy reach.

The walks are graded according to length: short (30–60 minutes), medium (60–90 minutes), or long (90–120 minutes). These timings are only approximate. The actual time taken for a particular walk will depend partly on the age and fitness of the walker and even more on the amount of time they devote to each of the sites along the way.

Ideally, the walks should be read and walked in the order that they were written and published, enabling each walk to inform those that follow it. Several of the walks deliberately overlap with others, revisiting the same sites in order to reveal new aspects of their history, allowing a more complex and layered picture to develop. This mirrors the stratified history of the area itself, in which places are, both metaphorically and literally, shaped by the accretion of successive ages.

However, each walk is also, so far as possible, intended to work as a self-contained experience. If the reader so wishes, the walks can be read in any order. Within each walk, some of the sites are accompanied by a cross-reference – for example, '(p 12)' would indicate that related information is to be found on page 12 – enabling the reader to build up a fuller picture of a particular place. The comprehensive index can also be used to cross-reference places and people. Indeed, by using the cross-references and index, readers can effectively create their own walks.

Anecdotal or explanatory notes are included as footnotes on the page to which they refer, signified by an asterisk (or cross, if there are two on the same page). References to sources are in the 'Notes' section at the end of the book.

Why?

Kings, Queens and Bishops, the great and the good, all feature on these walks. However, the walks pay special tribute to those who are generally consigned to the margins and footnotes of history – the immigrants and refugees, who brought new skills to the area*; the Irish 'navigators' who drained these marshes and the publicans who quenched their thirsts; craftsmen and tradesmen; Thames Watermen and unskilled labourers; doctors and nurses; rebels and reformers; all those who built this place with their sweat and toil – not forgetting the unknown dead who lie in its paupers' graveyards. And if some of the walks seem to give undue prominence to Bankside's actors, whores and outlaws – well, they do say the Devil has the best tunes, and this *is* The Outlaw Borough!

In the mid-17th Century, the Puritan regime, led by Oliver Cromwell, closed down the Bankside theatres, brothels, bear-pits and other dens of iniquity. The area was gradually taken over by craftsmen's workshops, timber yards, wharves and warehouses. By Victorian times The Borough contained some of the most deprived parts of London. During the latter half of the 20th Century, The South Bank at Waterloo developed as a citadel of culture. The rest of the south bank, badly bombed during The Blitz, had seemingly been abandoned to dereliction and decay.

Elephant and Castle shopping centre: mural by Kickstart/NRF (info@onitdesign.com)

The 'regeneration' of Bankside began in the 1980s. It gathered pace in the 90s and by the 21st Century was extending southwards, down through The Borough towards Elephant and

* Brewing, glass-blowing and pottery were but three local crafts benefiting from new techniques brought in by medieval refugees from the religious conflicts in Flanders. Here in Southwark, immigrants were free to practise their crafts and trades outside the restrictions imposed by Guilds within The City of London.

Castle. South of the river had become fashionable once again. The artists, musicians and party people who'd squatted or leased the wharves got pushed out by the property boom; old warehouses were gutted and refurbished as designer lofts or knocked down to make way for gated developments. It remains to be seen to what extent the new arrivals – whether living or working here, or just visiting – will feel a connection with the area's complex heritage.

Throughout its 2000-year history, this place has renewed itself with each new wave of settlers. No one wants it preserved in aspic. But nor would we wish to see its fabulous jumble of low-rise architectures bulldozed by one-size-fits-all glass and chrome towers. There are also warning signs that 'London's most historic borough' could turn into one vast theme park: the replica of Sir Francis Drake's ship The Golden Hind may be popular with children but has no actual connection with St Mary Overie dock in which it is moored[*].

How do we resist the 'theme-parking' of history? This book is, in part, a creative response to that question. I began conducting unusual walks as a way of connecting, and helping others connect, with the place I live – retrieving its 'secret histories', deciphering the hidden clues in back-streets and alleys, affirming the spirit of this special place. For me, the very act of walking these streets invites them to tell us their stories.

As a theatre-maker, I have been inspired by the history of this area, and my work has been widely performed in this same south London neighbourhood. The walks are themselves a kind of promenade performance – because history is more than the aggregate of all that has come before; more than the selective recall of names, dates, events: it's a stream of stories, some of which we're still in the process of telling.

Back in November 1996, I invited the theatre director Ken Campbell and other thespian friends to gather in the yard of The George Inn for a guided walk entitled 'The Mysteries Pilgrimage'.

---

[*] Conversely, it could be argued that such visitor attractions are entirely in keeping with Bankside's time-honoured role as London's entertainment district. The principal objection to such establishments is that they tend to obscure the particular story of an extraordinary place with their own generalised, 'homogenised' view of history.

SECRET BANKSIDE

My best-known published work, *The Southwark Mysteries*, could be said to have evolved out of that original walk. At the same time, the walk itself attracted a lot of interest, and I soon found myself commissioned to create others on specific themes. In this book I've written up some of my favourites, finishing with a short excursion to the site of William Blake's house in Lambeth. Although in written form, I hope to transmit something of the passion and playfulness that characterises the live walks.

The intention is that, equipped with this book and our imaginations, we will walk these streets and conjure these spirits of the past, present and future.

The author during a performance at the Cross Bones Graveyard

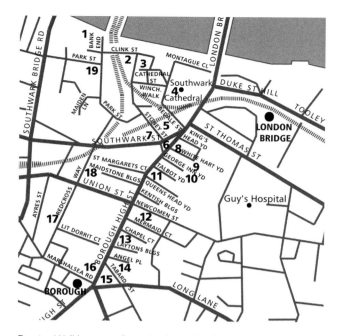

Route: *Walking away from the river with* **The Anchor Pub (1)** *on our right, turn immediately left under the railway arch along Clink Street, past the sites of the* **Clink prison (2)** *and* **Winchester Palace (3)** *to Southwark Cathedral (4). Turn right and go south through* **Borough Market (5)**. *Cross Southwark Street to the site of the* **Counter prison (6)**, *looking back at the* **Hop Exchange (7)** *before crossing Borough High Street to the site of* **The White Hart (8)**. *Coming back out of White Hart Yard, turn left and walk down the left-hand side of Borough High Street, visiting the yards of* **The George (9)** *and the former* **Tabard Inn (10)**. *Go past the site of* **The Queen's Head (11)**, *also on the left. Crossing Newcomen Street, continue down Borough High Street, past the former sites of the* **Marshalsea (12)** *and, a little further on, the* **King's Bench (13)** *and* **White Lion (14)** *prisons, to* **St George the Martyr Church (15)**. *Cross to the west side of Borough High Street, the old site of* **The Duke of Suffolk's Palace (16)**. *At the nearby traffic lights, turn right and walk west along Marshalsea Road, then take the second turning right up Redcross Way. A little up the road on the left are* **Red Cross Cottages and Garden (17)** *and, on the right, beyond the crossroads with Union Street, is the* **Cross Bones Graveyard (18)**. *Continue up Redcross Way, across Southwark Street, then take the left fork up Park Street. On the left is the* **plaque commemorating the 'international incident' (19)** *and, at the end of the road, The Anchor.*

The Outlaw Borough

This walk explores how the stories of Bankside and the nearby Borough were shaped by their location on the south bank, outside the law of The City of London. It's a tale of prisons – and of 'Liberties', including The Liberty of The Clink, where brothels were licensed by Bishops. In medieval London, such activities, whilst forbidden within The City, were permitted in designated areas outside the city walls or, as on Bankside, south of the river. The Borough was itself a haven for outlaws and prone to periodic outbreaks of Mob rule.

Walk begins and ends: *The Anchor pub, Bankside (Bank End, at the top of Park Street, by the river).*

Duration: *medium, 60–90 minutes.*

Transport links: *London Bridge underground and overground railway stations (5–10 minutes walk).*

BANKSIDE'S OLDEST SURVIVING TAVERN is **The Anchor (1)** on the Thames riverside. Back in the 15th century, when it was called The Castle-on-the-Hoop, it doubled as a brothel. During the 18th century, the brewer and local MP Henry Thrale and his wife Hester hosted a literary salon here. Their regulars included the actor David Garrick, playwright Oliver Goldsmith, and Dr Johnson, author of the first English Dictionary. Johnson sometimes lodged at The Anchor, where he wrote his *Lives of the English Poets* (1779–81). He even went on holiday with the Thrales, giving rise to rumours of a *ménage-à-trois*. When Henry Thrale died in 1781, Johnson helped arrange the sale of his brewery to the Barclays banking dynasty. Thrale's former manager, Perkins, was retained to oversee its expansion, and by 1810 Barclay and Perkins' Anchor brewery was producing nigh on a quarter of a million barrels a year. A plaque in Park Street at the back of the pub records the names of the local brewery's successive owners – Monger, Child, the Thrales, Barclay and Perkins – up to its purchase by the Courage Brewery, which took it over in 1955 and only closed in the 1970s.

The Anchor provides an excellent vantage point to survey The City just over the river, with St Paul's Cathedral away to our left, and to reflect on the proximity yet utter remoteness of these two worlds. For centuries, The City used its poor relation on the south bank as a dumping-ground for the things it preferred not to see, or allow, within its walls. 'Foul trades', such as leather-working, were pushed over the river to Bankside and Bermondsey; likewise brothels and theatres – and prisons. In the words of John Taylor, the 17th Century's self-styled 'Water Poet' (pp 32–3, 35):

Five jails or prisons are in Southwark place,
The Counter, once St Margaret's Church defaced,
The Marshalsea, The King's Bench and White Lion [...]
Then there's the Clink, where handsome lodgings be

Going away from the river, with the Anchor on our right, we turn immediately left, passing under the imposing Victorian railway-arch, into Clink Street. On our right, fronted by suitably ghoulish exhibits, is The Clink Museum. **The Clink prison (2)** dates back to the 12th Century, when it was connected by underground passageways to Winchester Palace at the far end of the street. Over the next six centuries the prison occupied various sites along the waterfront, housing prostitutes, heretics and religious dissenters. Its cold, damp cells, overcrowded and flea-ridden, provided an ideal breeding-ground for contagious diseases, including typhus, the often fatal 'jail-fever'. The Clink's very name came to be used as a slang expression for prison. It was eventually sacked and torched by the Mob during the Gordon Riots in 1780.

The outlaw spirit lingered long after the prison was gone. During the 1980s and 90s, Clink Street warehouses were used for illicit parties. The street has a claim to be the birthplace of Acid House music. Right up to the Millennium, the wharves were occupied on short lets as artists' and musicians' studios. That community was evicted *en masse* on the first day of the year 2000 to make way for luxury river-front flats. The former site of Backspace, the community drop-in centre and internet café, is now occupied by a branch of the ubiquitous Starbucks.

In the Middle Ages, Southwark's prisons were located within its 'Liberties', manors which lay outside the jurisdiction

'Remains of the great Hall of Winchester House as they appeared in 1820' from *The Gentleman's Magazine*

of The City. The Clink was one of five such manors, bounded to the west by Paris Garden; to the south and east were King's, Guildable and Great Liberty. These Liberties offered sanctuary for outlaws who managed to escape across the river. In 1327, King Edward III granted the Guildable Manor to the City of London 'that it cease to be a haven for criminals'. Even when Southwark's lawless manors were incorporated in 1550 (as Bridge Ward Without), The Clink Liberty and Paris Garden retained their independence – and their reputation for lax morals.

We walk up to the far (east) end of Clink Street. On our right is the ruin of **Winchester Palace (3)**, the London residence of the Bishop of Winchester from around 1140 until 1626. Only the west wall of the Great Hall, with its 14th-century Rose Window, remains.

The medieval Diocese of Winchester extended from the Thames to the Channel Islands; its Bishop was one of the most powerful men in the land. In 1107, the Bishop of Winchester was granted sole authority over The Liberty of The Clink, including its long-established brothels or 'stews'. The Bishop and his clergy came up with an ingenious way to impose some order on the Liberty, whilst making a modest profit from fines imposed on those who broke the rules (p 40).

The stews were regulated under Ordinances dating from 1161 'according to the old customs that have been used and accustomed there out of time of mind'. These Ordinances provide a fascinating record of the problems faced by the Bishop in policing his lawless Liberty. Some explicitly prohibit aggressive soliciting by the women:

> if any woman of the bordello [...] draw any man by his gown or by his hood or by any other thing she shall make a fine to the lord of twenty shillings.

Others show a commendable desire to protect such women from predatory pimps. One such 'item' establishes that the woman simply rents her room from the stewholder, or brothel-keeper, who has no other hold over her:

> a woman that lives by her body – provided she pays her dues, as old custom is, that is to say fourteen pence a week for her chamber [...] shall have free licence and liberty to come and go, without any interruption of the Stewholder.

Others now seem downright comical, such as the injunction against stewholders keeping nuns or married women in their stews *without informing the authorities*!

'A Common Whore' by Andrzej Klimowski, based on an early 17th-century woodcut

So it was that here, for the best part of 500 years, the world's oldest profession was effectively licensed by the Church. The Ordinances, instituted during the reign of King Henry II, were signed by Thomas Becket, the future Archbishop of Canterbury, who was then martyred in his own Cathedral and subsequently canonised.

The 'women of the bordello' could thus justifiably have claimed to have been licensed by a saint!

In the late 15th Century there were eighteen licensed brothels operating on Bankside. They were suppressed on the orders of Henry VIII, though many reopened during Elizabeth I's reign. An early 17th-century engraving depicts 'The Fish Pond House on Stewes Side' as an elegant, thriving establishment. The Manor House, known as Holland's Leaguer (pp 91–2) counted the Stuart King James I among its clients. In 1647, the Bankside stews, along with the bear-pits and theatres, were finally closed by the Puritans.

At the end of Clink Street, with Mary Overie dock to our left, we turn right into Cathedral Street, then left through the gate to **Southwark Cathedral (4)** (pp 40–2), formerly the Church of St Mary Overie. The name links the church with the ferryman's daughter who, according to legend, founded a Convent on the site in the year 606 (p 83), though it may simply refer to the Church of St Mary 'over the river'. The dedication is generally believed to have been to the Virgin Mary. It has also been suggested that the Mary in question was the Magdalen, whose ancient parish merged with St Margaret's in 1540 to form St Saviour's parish. During this period of the English Reformation, the church was likewise renamed St Saviour's Church, ending its association with a Catholic saint of dubious provenance, though it continued to minister to a congregation that included Bankside actors and whores.

The church had its share of hard times: it was even leased to a baker who used it as a pigsty. After the dissolution of the monasteries in 1539, the parishioners had to rent it from Henry VIII. In 1614, a group known as 'The Bargainers' bought the church from James I. From then until the 1890s it enjoyed a remarkable degree of independence, including the right to appoint its own ministers. In 1905 the parish church of St Saviour's also became the Cathedral for the new Anglican diocese of Southwark.

One of The Bargainers was Robert Harvard, friend of Shakespeare, high-street butcher and licensee of The Queen's Head, whose son John was baptised here in 1607. John Harvard gave his name to the American university, which he endowed, and to Southwark Cathedral's Harvard Chapel, the former Chapel of St John restored by members of Harvard University.

From the Harvard Chapel we can walk up to the retro-choir, in the east of the Cathedral behind the high altar, to view the remains of the 13th-century parish church – one of the earliest examples of Gothic architecture in London. The retro-choir houses The Lady Chapel and, a more recent addition, the Chapel of St Andrew: 'Dedicated to prayer for people who live or die under the shadow of HIV and AIDS'.

Crossing behind the high altar, we come to the tomb of Lancelot Andrewes, the last Bishop of Winchester to exercise authority in Southwark. He was a talented linguist: it was said that he would've been a good translator at the Tower of Babel! Further down the south aisle is the Shakespeare Monument – The Bard shown reclining against a Bankside backdrop featuring St Saviour's and The Globe – and, above, a stained-glass window depicting characters from his plays (p 41). Across the nave, over in the north aisle, is an imposing, brightly painted effigy of the medieval poet John Gower, portrayed with his head resting on the three books he wrote – in Latin, French and English. A nearby window shows Chaucer and his pilgrims setting off for Canterbury (pp 113, 115). Among the 15th-century roof-bosses displayed close to the west door is an image of the Devil devouring Judas Iscariot.

Coming out of Cathedral Yard, we head south under the railway viaduct that coils round the Cathedral like a giant serpent, or like that mythical creature whose name is preserved in Green Dragon Court. We enter the Victorian wrought-iron arcade that is **Borough Market (5)**. There has been a market in the vicinity since early medieval times. In 1462, Edward IV granted a Royal Charter to the Southwark Fair, otherwise known as Margaret's Fair or The Lady Fair, which was held every year from the 7th to the 9th of September. Kentish drovers, farmers and market-gardeners converged on St Margaret's Hill (the Borough High Street approach to London Bridge) to trade their produce and livestock. The fair also attracted strolling players, musicians and street entertainers, as well as the inevitable prostitutes and pickpockets. The chaotic scene is recorded by Hogarth in his painting 'Southwark Fair'. In 1762, after 300 rowdy years, the fair was banned as 'an affront to the dignity of London'. The wholesale fruit and vegetable stalls relocated to Borough Market. Traders continued to deal in bushels and

The Hop Exchange, Southwark Street

pecks, and to enjoy early-morning drinking in local pubs like The Market Porter, which still does a roaring trade on Stoney Street, facing the market. In the early years of the 21st Century, Borough Market successfully reinvented itself as London's most prestigious farmers' market.

Emerging from the Market (either left down Bedale Street or Stoney Street, or through the main market-hall entrance), we cross the busy intersection of Southwark Street with Borough High Street. Standing in the fork between the two streets, we are on the site of St Margaret's Church and **The Counter (6)**, or Compter, prison. During the Reformation, the old Catholic church was requisitioned for use as a court and prison. It was destroyed during the Great Fire of Southwark in 1676. The prison moved to Tooley Street, a hundred metres north-west, though the name survives here in the dark, narrow alley linking the two main thoroughfares.

Looking back, we see the north-west side of Southwark Street dominated by the imposing **Hop Exchange (7)**. It was built in 1866 with a glass roof to enable traders to examine the hops by natural light. Over the other way, across Borough High Street, is the sienna-coloured May Hop Factors building, another reminder of the importance of brewing, not only to celebrated dynasties like the Thrales but to all classes of Southwark people. Well into the middle of the 20th Century, entire neighbourhoods would go hop-picking in Kent at the end of August.

Borough High Street, formerly St Margaret's Hill, was described by the 17th-century playwright Thomas Dekker as 'one continued ale-house'. A survey of 1631 listed 288 ale-houses, 43 of which were closed down on the grounds of plague or rowdiness. In his *Travels through more than thirty times twelve signs*, John Taylor the Water Poet dedicates a piece of doggerel to the inn-signs of more than 360 local taverns:

> Although these Harts do never run away,
> They'll tire a Man to hunt them every day;
> The Game and Chase is good for Recreation,
> But dangerous to make't an occupation.

We cross Borough High Street to enter the alley called White Hart Yard: a bronze plaque identifies this as the site of **The White Hart (8)**, the tavern immortalised in the works of Shakespeare (p 42) and Dickens – not to mention John Taylor!

In 1450 Jack Cade, leader of a Kentish rebel army, established his headquarters here. Like his predecessor Wat Tyler, Cade ordered his men to sack the Marshalsea prison, freeing the prisoners to swell their ranks. When the Mob stormed London Bridge, the King fled to Kenilworth Castle in the Midlands. The people of Southwark at first welcomed Cade as a liberator, but Mob rule rapidly descended into terror. At the height of the insurgency, decapitated heads were paraded on poles and mockingly made to kiss one another. Small wonder that his supporters, taking advantage of a general amnesty, deserted as rapidly as they had once flocked to join him. The King's revenge was swift and gruesome: Jack Cade's head joined those of other traitors above the south gate of London Bridge.

Back in the days when this was the only bridge over the Thames, pilgrims and other travellers making their way from The City to the South East and the Continent would cross over before the drawbridge was raised at sundown. They would spend the night in one of Southwark's many coaching inns, then set off at dawn. The east side of Borough High Street is intersected by the alleys and yards of those old travellers' inns, most of which have long since vanished.

Coming back out of White Hart Yard, we turn left onto Borough High Street and left again into the yard of **The George (9)**, the last galleried coaching-inn left in London. There was an inn here when Geoffrey Chaucer slept next door at The Tabard. The George burnt down in the Great Fire of Southwark in 1676 – more devastating than the famous Great Fire of London, which occurred ten years earlier, but then The Borough's dead were poor, dispensable and easily forgotten. The inn was rebuilt, with wooden balconies overlooking a courtyard with stables. The stables have gone, the courtyard is now shared with modern offices and wine bars, but the black-and-white timbered building of 1676 has survived, complete with its wooden galleries.

Coming out of The George, turn left down Borough High Street, taking the first left into Talbot Yard, the next yard south of The George. This is the site of **The Tabard (10)** (pp 113, 115), the inn where Chaucer's Pilgrims gather in *The Canterbury Tales*. During the Middle Ages the art of brewing was perfected in Southwark; refugees from Flanders introduced new techniques and recipes. In *The Canterbury Tales*, Chaucer remarks on the strength of the local brews. Before embarking on his famously obscene tale, the Miller warns his prospective audience:

> And if the words get muddled in my tale
> Just put it down to too much Southwark ale.

Coming out of Talbot Yard, we again turn left into Borough High Street, and, staying on the left side, walk down past the former **Queen's Head** tavern **(11)** at 103 Borough High Street, on the corner of Queen's Head Yard. This was the birthplace of John Harvard (p 21), benefactor of the American university that bears his name. Look out for the plaque below the ground-floor bay window.

Throughout its turbulent history, the authorities regularly sought to impose some order on the Outlaw Borough. In 1374 King Edward III issued an edict requiring

> the good men of Southwark to build in our Royal Street which extends from the Church of the Blessed Margaret towards the South a certain House for the safe custody of the prisoners of the Marshalsea.

The **Marshalsea prison (12)** (pp 50–1) was originally situated on the east side of Borough High Street, between Newcomen Street and Mermaid Court. It took its name from the ancient

Court of the Knights Marshal, which travelled with the King and had jurisdiction over any area in which he spent the night. Along with debtors and petty criminals, the prison also housed prisoners of conscience. John Marbeck the organist was imprisoned here in 1543 for secretly compiling an English concordance to the Bible. In Queen Mary's reign, many Protestants were crammed into 'Bonner's coal-hole', an underground dungeon named after the Catholic Bishop of London. When Elizabeth I came to the throne, Edmund Bonner soon found himself thrown in his own coal-hole. In 1753 John Wesley condemned the Marshalsea as 'a nursery of all manner of wickedness. Oh shame to men that there should be such a place, such a picture of hell on earth'.

The **King's Bench prison (13)** also dates back to the 14th Century. Until the mid-18th Century it occupied a site a little further down Borough High Street, on the same side, just north of Angel Place. Thomas Dekker, who depicted London low-life in plays like *The Honest Whore,* was imprisoned for debt in the King's Bench from 1613 to 1616. Another 17th-century prisoner, Geoffrey Minshul, wrote:

> A prison is a grave to bury men alive [...] It is a Microcosmos, a little world of woe, it is a map of misery [...] It is a place that hath more diseases dominant in it, than the pest-house in the plague-time, and it stinks more than the Lord Mayor's dog house.

In 1758 the King's Bench relocated a short distance south to St George's Fields, close to what is now Stones End Street (pp 45–6). A decade later, when John Wilkes the Outlaw MP returned from exile in France, he was arrested and detained there. His presence in The Borough only served to excite the revolutionary fervour of the Mob, who escorted him to prison with cries of 'Wilkes and Liberty'. When they refused to disperse, government troops opened fire. This so-called 'Massacre of St George's Fields' almost started an English Revolution. The Mob stormed over London Bridge into The City, burning and looting, and even laid siege to King George III's palace. Yet within a decade, Wilkes had been assimilated into the British establishment. In 1780, when the Gordon Rioters (p 123) rampaged through Southwark, it was Lord Mayor Wilkes who called in the militia.

We walk on down Borough High Street to the John Harvard Library on Angel Place, the site of the **White Lion prison (14)**. Southwark's prisons regularly changed location, incorporating other buildings to increase their capacity. From around 1540 the White Lion Inn was commandeered as the Surrey County Jail. In 1811, a new Marshalsea prison (pp 50–1) was built on the site of the former King's Bench and White Lion prisons, close to the Church of **St George the Martyr (15)** (pp 50, 78–9) with its striking white stone tower.

Across the road, facing the front of the church, a modern brick building now stands on the corner with Marshalsea Road, on the site of the **Duke of Suffolk's Palace (16)**. For a time the Palace housed a Royal Mint, which gave its name to the notorious thieves' quarter – as in 'Matt of the Mint', a character from John Gay's *The Beggar's Opera*. During his father's imprisonment in the Marshalsea for debt, the young Charles Dickens took lodgings nearby, walking to work through The Mint (pp 49–50).

At the junction, turn right and walk west along Marshalsea Road. Take the second turn right and head north up Redcross Way, a long straight road, framed by a railway arch in the distance, which runs parallel with Borough High Street through the heart of the old Mint. When Charles Booth was conducting his survey of London poverty in the 1890s, his researcher George Duckworth described The Mint as

> a set of courts and small streets which for number, viciousness, poverty and crowding, is unrivalled in anything I have hitherto seen in London.

Duckworth explored the area with a policeman who warned him: 'Police don't go down here unless they have to, and never singly.'

About a hundred metres up Redcross Way, on the left, is a terrace of beautiful, distinctly rural-looking cottages fronted by a communal garden. **Red Cross Cottages and Garden (17)** (p 121) were the work of Octavia Hill, a Victorian social-housing reformer and co-founder of the National Trust, who believed that the only way to improve the behaviour of London's poor was to offer them decent living conditions. She acquired this site in the

Redcross Cottages and Garden

1880s, when it was a derelict paper factory. It took weeks to clear the rotting paper and even longer for the smell of bonfires to disperse. Here Octavia established six model-dwelling cottages with a communal hall and garden. Her tenants were subject to strict terms and conditions: drinking, swearing and defaulting on rent payments were all grounds for eviction. In return, they got to live in cottages that must have been the envy of their slum-dwelling neighbours.

We go straight across the crossroads at Union Street, continuing up Redcross Way. On our right is a vacant plot, currently being used a works depot. The rusty iron gate to the site has been turned into a shrine. This is **Cross Bones (18)** (pp 79–81, 120–1), an unconsecrated graveyard dating from medieval times. Tudor historian John Stow refers to it as a burial ground for 'single women' – a euphemism for the prostitutes who worked in Bankside's legal 'stews'. There's a bitter irony here: such women were condemned to be buried in unhallowed ground, despite being licensed by the Church.

In Victorian times, Cross Bones witnessed many a pauper's burial. It was also the haunt of body-snatchers, seeking specimens for the anatomy classes held at nearby Guy's Hospital. The graveyard was finally closed in 1853, on the grounds that it was 'completely overcharged with dead' and that 'further burials' would be 'inconsistent with a due regard for the public health and public decency'. The graveyard slept peacefully for the best part of a century. Then in the 1990s, prior to work on the Jubilee Line Extension, Museum of London archaeologists conducted a partial excavation of the site, removing 148 skeletons. By their estimate, these represented less than 1% of the total burials.

Local people are campaigning for part of this historic burial ground to be rededicated as a memorial garden. Cross Bones is a symbol both of the secret history of the Outlaw Borough, which is unearthed wherever developers sink foundations for new buildings, and of the tenacity of that history, its ability to reinvent itself in the living culture of the inner city.

To complete this circular walk, we cross Southwark Street, continuing up Redcross Way, then veer to the left up Park Street. Set into a wall on the left-hand side, an intriguing plaque (19) announces: 'An International Incident Occurred Here, 1850'. This is a reference to the humiliation of Baron von Haynau, the 'Austrian Butcher', also known as 'The Hyena'. 1848 had been the year of revolutions across Europe. Von Haynau had been responsible for the particularly brutal suppression of the Hungarian uprising. He was invited to London by the Westminster political élite, but made the mistake of venturing south of the river. During his visit to the Barclay and Perkin's brewery, the draymen pelted him with horse dung and chased him through the streets of The Borough. The Baron hid in a dustbin in the yard of The George but was soon discovered and subjected to further abuse. He was eventually rescued by the police and ferried away to safety on the north bank. The event is celebrated in a Bankside ballad of the time:

Turn him out, turn him out, from our side of the Thames.
Let him go to great Tories and high-titled dames.
He may walk the West End and parade in his pride,
But he'll not come back again near The George in
    Bankside.

Carry on up Park Street, through what was once Deadman's Place, and we're back where we began, at The Anchor by the river.

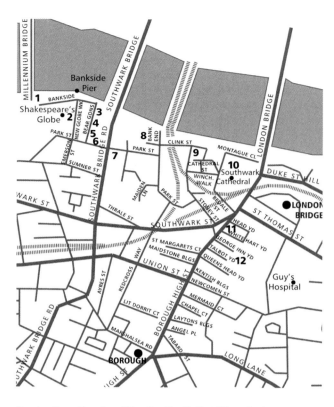

Route: *From the site of* The Cardinal's Hat (**1**) *walk downstream along Bankside, with the river on our left, past* Shakespeare's Globe (**2**). *Turn right by the* Ferryman's Seat (**3**) *down* Bear Gardens (**4**), *past the site of* The Hope (**5**). *Walk to the end of the road, then turn left into Park Street, past the sites of* The Rose (**6**) *and* The Globe (**7**). *Turn left by* The Anchor (**8**) *and immediately right down Clink Street, past* Winchester Palace (**9**) *to* Southwark Cathedral (**10**). *Go through Cathedral Yard, up the steps, turn right down Borough High Street, crossing the road to the yards of* The White Hart (**11**) *and* The George (**12**).

Shakespeare's Bankside

This walk evokes the world of Shakespeare and his contemporaries. Theatres came south to Bankside for the same reason the brothels did: because they were forbidden in The City on the north bank. So it was that Shakespeare's plays came to be written and performed, not in the rarefied atmosphere of a university, still less in provincial Stratford, but in a riotous red-light district.

Walk begins: *facing Cardinal's Cap Alley, Bankside, between Shakespeare's Globe and the Millennium Bridge.*
  Ends: *The George, 77 Borough High Street.*

Duration: *short, 30–60 minutes.*

Transport links: *Southwark underground; London Bridge underground and overground railway stations (each 10–15 minutes walk).*

LONDON'S FIRST PURPOSE-BUILT PLAYHOUSES, The Theatre and The Curtain, date from 1576. They were in Shoreditch to the north – and outside the walls – of The City of London. By the end of the 16th Century, they had been joined by The Fortune in the Finsbury Liberty, a designated area also outside the City walls, and, here on Bankside, by The Rose, The Swan, The Globe and The Hope. The location of all these theatres, beyond the jurisdiction of The City proper, was no accident. In Shakespeare's time, theatres, along with bear-pits and brothels – or 'stews' – were forbidden within the City walls. In the eyes of its moral guardians, actors and whores were natural bedfellows, both equally liable to deprave its citizens. The Lord Mayor even petitioned the Queen's Privy Council to ban all plays, so as to protect 'our apprentices and servants' from such corrupting influences.

However, The City's writ did not run south of the river, where the independent manors of Paris Garden and The Liberty of The Clink (pp 19–20) coalesced to form Bankside, that waterfront strip of theatres, bear-pits, taverns and stews. Perhaps some of those City Fathers even saw the wisdom of having such a place of licence conveniently situated just across the river. Certainly there was always a thriving ferry trade to cater for a gentleman in search of forbidden pleasures. Once over here, however, he'd have to watch his step. The Bankside was a chaotic, dangerous place, a warren of dark alleyways where cut-purses and 'cony-catchers' lurked. Disembarking at night, our City gent may well have needed a guide to show him around. And who better than the ferryman who rowed him over, that noble precursor of the London cabbie?

Let us then, on this walk, invoke the spirit of John Taylor the Water Poet (1580–1653), Thames ferryman and incontinent writer of doggerel. Taylor had the knack of finding poetry in the most unlikely places. Some of his ditties were inspired by inn-signs observed on his epic Bankside pub-crawls:

> We are much better pleas'd with the bare Signe
> Than with the Hat or Card'nale – There's good Wine.

Our walk begins here at the site of **The Cardinal's Hat (1)**, Number 49 Bankside, next door to what is now the Provost's Lodging. The two houses are separated by the narrow Cardinal's Cap Alley. In the Protestant England of Taylor's day, the Catholic Cardinal would have been a figure of fun, if not outright contempt, though the insulting pub-name goes back to the Middle Ages. In fact, there had been a Cardinal's Hat on Bankside since at least 1361. During the next three centuries, it regularly appears on lists of licensed brothels, surviving the various attempts of Tudor monarchs to suppress the stews. In 1468 the Prior of Merton obtained The Cardinal's Hat in exchange for The Pope's Head, another brothel situated a few hundred metres to the south-east in Borough High Street. By James I's reign, however, The Cardinal's Hat had become a relatively respectable hostelry.

Standing with our backs to the river, on our left is Shakespeare's Globe, an impressive replica of The Globe theatre, which stood roughly a hundred metres south-east of here. In 1613, the theatre burnt down when a spark from a cannon fired during a performance of *Henry VIII* set fire to the thatched roof. There were no casualties, although 'one man had his breeches set on fire, that would perhaps have broiled him, if he had not by the benefit of a provident wit put it out with bottle-ale'. Rumours soon spread of plans to rebuild the theatre on the north bank.

Shakespeare's Globe

The Thames Watermen, alarmed at the damaging effects such a move might have on the ferry trade, protested. Our man John Taylor, having published a pamphlet entitled 'The Cause of the Watermen's Suit Concerning Players', led a delegation to put their case to the Globe actors. They met here at The Cardinal's Hat. The Watermen's petition was not well received. One of the actors is said to have sarcastically inquired whether the Watermen would like them to move St Paul's Cathedral over to the Bankside, in order to encourage more ferry crossings. In the event, The Globe was rebuilt on the same site, where it remained until it was closed by the Puritans in 1642 and demolished two years later. Nonetheless, the Watermen suspected that Taylor had double-crossed them. He later wrote that it was

> reported that I took bribes from the players to let the suit fail and that I had supper with them at the Cardinal's Hat on the Bankside [...] Vipers! Ignorant knaves! Unthankful villains!

Shakespeare's Globe (2) was erected on its new site here on Bankside using traditional Elizabethan building methods and materials. It owes its existence to the conviction and energy of the American actor Sam Wanamaker, who overcame the intransigence of the local authority and the mockery of the English theatre establishment to realise his vision. On 23 April 1993, John Gielgud dedicated the theatre; its first season was inaugurated four years later with a production of *Henry V*.

'The Bear Garden' (left) and 'The Globe Theatre' (right) based on a 17th-century woodcut, 'Engraved for the Encyclopedia Londinensis 1825'

Looking upstream from here we can see the red-painted Blackfriars Bridge. The Swan theatre was situated on the south bank, close to where the bridge now stands. Erected in 1595 by Francis Langley, a goldsmith, money-lender and theatrical entrepreneur, The Swan was the second theatre on Bankside, following the establishment of The Rose eight years before. Such theatres were identified not only by name but also by the totemic emblems hung outside them in the manner of inn-signs. Johannes de Witt, writing in 1596, hailed the one with 'the sign of the swan' as the 'largest and most magnificent' of all the London amphitheatres, noting that it could accommodate 3000 people. However, perhaps hampered by not having a resident company, it proved unable to compete with The Rose and the other playhouses on the north bank. It was closed in 1597, following a performance of Jonson and Nashe's allegedly seditious play *The Isle of Dogs.* Two years later, as part of a clampdown on satirical and radical writings, Nashe's works were burned and an edict was issued that they should never again be reprinted. All traces of The Swan have long since vanished, though we'll be visiting the site on our 'Tate To Elephant' walk. It's also only a short walk from Shakespeare's Globe to the former sites of The Hope, The Rose and The Globe.

Walking downstream, with the river on our left, turn right by the worn, stone **Ferryman's Seat (3)** down **Bear Gardens (4)**. Bear-baiting was a popular amusement on Bankside, closely linked with the theatre and brothel trades. Here, in 1613, Philip

Henslowe converted his bear-pit so that it could double as a theatre, which he renamed **The Hope (5)**. His son-in-law was Edward Alleyn, the actor-manager and bear-baiting promoter. In 1604 both men were appointed Masters of the Royal Bears, Bulls and Mastiffs. The amphitheatres of The Rose and The Globe resembled the nearby circular bear-pits. Indeed, in the famous 'Long View of London' by 17th-century Czech artist Wenceslaus Hollar, The Globe and 'The Bear-baiting' (The Hope) are mistakenly transposed (see frontispiece). The proximity of bear-pits to the Bankside theatres helps us appreciate the power of Shakespeare's curious stage direction: 'Exit pursued by a bear.' The sudden appearance of a bear, whether real or played by an actor in a bear-skin, would surely have unleashed pandemonium among the groundlings at The Globe.

Our guide, John Taylor, was a quarrelsome character, much given to taking on unusual wagers: he once attempted to row up the Thames in a paper boat using fish tied to sticks as oars. When a rival claimed to be 'the King's rhyming poet', Taylor challenged him to a trial of 'dainty conceits' at The Hope. In the event, the 'rhyming rascal', as Taylor dubbed him, failed to appear. Our Water Poet even had a play performed at The Hope, though by his own admission it was not a great hit:

O twas that foolish scurvy play
At Hope that took his sense away.

A more successful première was Ben Jonson's *Bartholomew Fair* which opened at The Hope in 1614. The remains of The Hope were discovered here in Bear Gardens in 2001, though the theatre's footprint is hidden under more recent developments.

The playwright John Fletcher lodged nearby in Addison's Rents, a tenement row adjoining Bear Gardens and Unicorn Alley. There was much gossip concerning his relationship with his collaborator Francis Beaumont: that they lived together 'sharing everything in the closest intimacy' – even a mistress! – though the suggestion was more that they were gay lovers; and that 'in their joint plays their talents are so […] completely merged into one, that the hand of Beaumont cannot be clearly distinguished from that of Fletcher'. After Beaumont's death, Fletcher became linked with Philip Massinger, another dramatist. Massinger and Fletcher were eventually buried together in Southwark Cathedral.

Fletcher also lodged at The Unicorn, a nearby tavern and stew, which in 1597 had been leased by Philip Henslowe. It was later acquired by Edward Alleyn, who was married to Henslowe's step-daughter, Joan Woodward. Joan was herself imprisoned in The Clink (p 18), and paraded in a cart as the keeper of a bawdy house. After her death, Alleyn married Constance, daughter of John Donne the poet and Dean of St Paul's. Their marriage settlement included The Unicorn and three other brothels: The Barge, The Bell and The Cock. All have long since vanished, along with Addison's rents and Unicorn Alley. Bear Gardens and Rose Alley remain, recalling Bankside's Elizabethan glory days.

At the bottom end of Bear Gardens, turn left into Park Street. On our left, just past Rose Alley, is the site of **The Rose (6)**, Bankside's first theatre, built by that same Philip Henslowe in 1587. Having parted company with The Lord Chamberlain's Men (later known as The King's Men), Henslowe established his own Lord Admiral's Men as the resident company at The Rose. As was customary at the time, these companies of actors took their names from their aristocratic patrons. Such patronage provided a measure of protection from the draconian vagrancy laws under which actors were often harassed.

It was at The Rose that Edward Alleyn created the lead roles in the ground-breaking tragedies of Christopher Marlowe. Shakespeare was almost certainly inspired by seeing a production of *Tamburlaine* here. Marlowe's masterful use of the iambic pentameter, the ten-syllable line with the stress on alternating syllables, strongly influenced Shakespeare's own writing, including *Titus Andronicus*, which also played at The Rose. It's not known exactly when young Will first arrived in London. He had evidently made his mark by 1592, provoking Robert Greene's envious attack on him as 'an upstart crow, beautified with our feathers'.

In 1593, aged 28, Marlowe was murdered in a tavern in Deptford, allegedly in an argument over 'the reckoning', though some claim he was assassinated. His radical thinking and unconventional lifestyle had aroused the interest of the authoritarian Elizabethan state. He had been accused of many things – including preaching atheism and practising sodomy.

Marlowe's *Doctor Faustus* and *The Jew of Malta,* Thomas Kyd's *The Spanish Tragedy* and Shakespeare's *Henry VI Part One* were among the other plays performed at The Rose. Those who regarded all such plays as 'the cause of Sin' were especially concerned that the pretty boys who played the heroines would arouse homosexual desires among the men in the audience. Prior to the Restoration, women were not allowed to perform on stage. An exception was Mary Frith, alias Moll Cutpurse, immortalised by Dekker and Middleton in their play *The Roaring Girl.* Moll herself appeared on stage in other plays and may well have been the first professional English actress. She performed male roles, reversing the common practice of boy actors playing female parts. Even offstage, she wore men's breeches and smoked a pipe. Moll supplemented her acting work by 'fencing' stolen goods. We also know she enjoyed a drink. In 1612, her enforced penance at St Paul's Cross was reported thus:

> Moll Cutpurse, a notorious baggage who used to go about in men's apparel [...] seemed very penitent; but it is since doubted that she was maudlin drunk, being discovered to have tippled of three quarters of sack before she came to her penance.

'Doubted', in this archaic usage, means 'suspected' or 'feared'; Moll's tears of penitence were evidently brought on by the drink. She sounds like our sort of Roaring Girl! Let's invite her to tag along with John Taylor on this stroll around Bankside.

Sam Wanamaker's efforts to establish Bankside as a theatrical heritage site received a boost when the remains of The Rose, then The Globe, were discovered here, close to Southwark Bridge. The Rose's foundations were unearthed in 1989, during an archaeological dig prior to the redevelopment of the site. Thanks to a campaign led by many eminent thespians, the developers' plans were modified, enabling the remains to be preserved in the basement of the new building. Nevertheless, the entombing of the theatre inside an anonymous concrete shell was regarded by many as a tragedy in itself.

With The Rose on our left we continue along Park Street, which passes under Southwark Bridge Road. On our right is the site of **The Globe (7)**, marked by a bronze plaque and display-boards. Originally called simply 'The Theatre', it had been built in Shoreditch in 1576 for the carpenter James Burbage, who also owned The Curtain. When the ground lease was due to expire in 1598, the landlord Giles Allen attempted to repossess The Theatre, thereby acquiring a free purpose-built playhouse. He met his match in James' sons Cuthbert and Richard Burbage and their Lord Chamberlain's Men. They came with armed workmen to remove The Theatre on 28 December. Under the supervision of master carpenter Peter Streete, they dismantled the timber frame, carted it over London Bridge – some say they ferried it over the river – reassembled it on Bankside, and renamed it The Globe.

The story of the Lord Chamberlain's Men dragging the frame of the theatre over the frozen Thames is now generally regarded as apocryphal, though it seems plausible enough. Before the embankments were built the river was both wider and shallower than it is today. Over the centuries London Bridge has been demolished and rebuilt – not once, but many times. During the reign of Elizabeth I, it was built up with houses jutting out over the river (p 85). The supports of the bridge restricted the flow of water, often causing it to freeze over in winter. Denied their usual source of income, the ferrymen would set up booths on the ice, serving food and drink to those who came either to skate or in search of other amusements, thus establishing the tradition of 'Frost Fairs'.

Following The Globe's reconstruction on Bankside, Shakespeare acquired a one-eighth stake in the theatre. His fellow 'householders' were Richard and Cuthbert Burbage, four other members of the Lord Chamberlain's company, and the owner of the land on which the theatre stood. *Hamlet, Othello, King Lear* and many other Shakespeare plays had their premières here at The Globe. The roles of Hamlet and other tragic heroes were created by Richard Burbage, the young actor who came to rival even the great Alleyn.

Walk straight on to the junction at the end of the road. In fact, Park Street continues, veering sharply to the right. On our left is Bank End, a short road leading up to the river and **The Anchor (8)** pub, formerly The Castle-on-the-Hoop, one of Bankside's original licensed stews. There has been a tavern on this site since medieval times. In 1599, Shakespeare apparently rented lodgings in the Liberty of the Clink, only a short walk away from where The Globe was being reconstructed on Bankside. The main evidence for this is an entry in the Bishop of Winchester's records, showing that he'd defaulted on his rates! However, given the controversy surrounding Shakespeare's identity, it is hard to be more specific than H E Popham – regarding whether The Bard ever drank at The Anchor:

> He should have come here. He must have come here. Let us say, finally and definitely, that he did.

Bank End and the adjoining part of Park Street used to be called Deadman's Place. The ominous name has spawned a local legend that it was once the site of a gallows. There was subsequently a Dissenters' burial ground here (p 92), although 'Deadman' may simply be a corruption of the name of a local landlord. Many of the rents and yards in this area took their names from the owners of the properties. When Shakespeare was lodging hereabouts, the Bankside was a narrow ribbon of theatres, taverns, stews and cheap rents along this stretch of the south bank, with another ribbon of inns running down the High Street as far as the Church of St George the Martyr. All around was open country – woods and fields, fish-ponds and tenter-grounds. During the 17th Century this area became more industrialised, with glassworks operating in the vicinity of Deadman's Place alongside breweries, water-mills, wharves and craft workshops.

The last part of this walk follows the same route as the first part of 'The Outlaw Borough' walk (pp 18–22) – this time focusing on Shakespearean associations with The Liberty of The Clink. From Bank End, looking up towards the river and with The Anchor to our left, we turn right under the railway arch and past the Clink Prison Museum. Walk east along Clink Street to the far end. On our right are the skeletal remains of **Winchester Palace (9)**, the London house of the Bishop of Winchester. In 1424 a feast was held here to celebrate the marriage of the niece of the incumbent Bishop, Cardinal Beaufort, to King James I of Scotland. Beaufort, bastard son of John of Gaunt, is best remembered as the man who presided over the burning of Joan of Arc. In Shakespeare's *Henry VI Part One* he is portrayed as a corrupt, political schemer. Gloucester does not mince words:

> Thou that givest whores indulgences to sin:
> […]
> Winchester goose! […]
> Thee I'll chase hence, thou wolf in sheep's array.

This is a reference to the Bishop of Winchester's right to license the brothels, or 'stews', of the Liberty (pp 19–21); the women who worked in them became known as the 'Winchester Geese'. (Why Geese? The white of their aprons and/or their bare breasts, when seen from the river, has been suggested as one explanation.) Shakespeare's *Troilus and Cressida* also refers to a 'Goose of Winchester', and being 'bitten by Winchester Geese' was a common euphemism for catching a sexually transmitted disease.

Many learned academics have speculated on Shakespeare's sources; his erudition is often cited as evidence that only a courtier like Sir Francis Bacon could have written the plays. No one would deny The Bard's extraordinary command of language and dramatic form, nor his intimate knowledge of court life, but this should not blind us to the fact that he was equally at home with the vernacular and the lives of the common people. Is it too fanciful to imagine that Will came across, say, the tragic love-story of Romeo and Juliet not in some obscure Italian text but as told by a sailor in a Bankside tavern, or perhaps even by a Winchester Goose in a Bankside stew? Shakespeare's delight in explicit language and bawdy humour would certainly have appealed to those members of his audience who were as much at home in a brothel as in a theatre.

We're now at the eastern end of Clink Street. To our left is the river and St Mary Overie dock (p 83). Ahead is **Southwark Cathedral (10)**, formerly St Saviour's and, before that, the Church of St Mary Overie. We veer right, following Cathedral Street round, and enter the Cathedral by the west door. The names of

The Shakespeare monument in Southwark Cathedral

more than half the actors listed in Shakespeare's First Folio also appear in St Saviour's parish records. The actor Edward Alleyn was a church warden. His father-in-law – the ubiquitous theatre impresario, bear-baiter and brothel-keeper Philip Henslowe – was one of The Bargainers (p 21) who bought the church from James I in 1614. Henslowe died the following year and was buried in the chancel.

The Shakespeare Monument, in the south aisle, has a statue of the playwright reclining in front of a relief, based on Hollar's 'Long View of London' (see frontispiece), which shows the church, The Globe and other Bankside landmarks. Above, a stained-glass window depicts characters from Shakespeare's plays. Another window, which was shattered during a World War II bombing raid, portrayed the (supposedly) gay dramatists Fletcher and Massinger, who are also buried here. There is speculation that Shakespeare himself was bisexual. Some of his sonnets were written for a man, although the mysterious 'Dark Lady', to whom some of them are addressed, may have been Luce Morgan, the African Madame of a Clerkenwell brothel.

Shakespeare's brother Edmund was buried in the Cathedral on New Year's Eve 1607 'with a forenoon knell of the great bell'. Funerals were generally conducted in the afternoon. Edmund's fellow actors paid twenty shillings – ten times the going rate – to have the service conducted in the morning, so that they could attend his funeral before performing in the afternoon.

Despite the close connections between the church and the theatre, relations were not always harmonious. In 1547,

Gardiner, the then Bishop of Winchester, protested that the Bankside actors were competing with his 'solemn mass' for Henry VIII by performing 'a solemn play, to try who shall have the most resort, they in game or I in earnest'.

The last Bishop of Winchester to exercise jurisdiction over Southwark was Lancelot Andrewes, whose tomb can be seen in the south choir. One of his sermons, on the theme of fighting a just war, may have influenced Shakespeare's version of the King's rousing St Crispin's Day speech before the Battle of Agincourt in *Henry V.*

Leaving the Cathedral by the west door, turn left, go through Cathedral Yard and up the steps, then turn right and walk down Borough High Street, past the front entrance to Borough Market. Cross at the traffic lights to White Hart Yard, the site of **The White Hart inn (11)** (pp 24, 51), former temporary headquarters of the 15th-century rebel Jack Cade. Like his predecessor Wat Tyler, Cade had led his Kentish army into Southwark, where they immediately set about sacking the prisons and freeing the inmates to swell their ranks. In Shakespeare's *Henry VI Part Two,* a messenger warns the King of the rampaging mob:

> Jack Cade hath almost gotten London Bridge:
> [...]
> The rascal people, thirsting after prey,
> Join with the traitor; and they jointly swear
> To spoil the city and your royal court.

Cade's triumph was short-lived. The battle for London Bridge raged throughout the night of 5 July 1450 but was inconclusive. The atrocities enacted by the rebel army in the name of Liberty soon alienated all but the most extreme factions. At a peace council convened in St Margaret's Church just across the road (p 23), a general amnesty was offered to any rebel who laid down his arms. In Shakespeare's play, Jack Cade laments:

> Hath my sword therefore broke through London gates, that you should leave me at the White Hart in Southwark?

On 13 July 1450, Jack Cade's naked corpse was formally identified by the landlady of The White Hart. It was then decapitated, quartered and paraded around the streets of Southwark. The head was impaled on a spike at Traitor's Gate.

We end this walk next door at **The George (12)** – not just because it's another of those inns to which Shakespeare 'must have come', but because, long before and long after the heyday of the Bankside playhouses, the yards of such coaching-inns were used for open-air performances of plays, their wooden galleries creating a rudimentary auditorium. Even in the 20th Century, prior to the reconstruction of Shakespeare's Globe, The George was an important local venue for seasonal productions of Shakespeare's work.

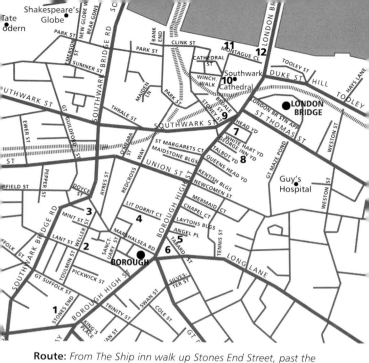

Route: *From The Ship inn walk up Stones End Street, past the site of the* King's Bench prison *(***1***). At the top of the street, turn left into Great Suffolk Street, then first right up Toulmin Street to* Lant Street *(***2***). Cross the road, go up Weller Street and in through the side entrance to Mint Street park, the former site of the* Mint Street Workhouse *(***3***). Turn right and walk along the main concourse to exit the park, turning right again onto Marshalsea Road. To the north of here was the area once known as* The Mint *(***4***). Walk east along Marshalsea Road, crossing at the next major junction to the Church of St George the Martyr. To the north of the church is St George's Gardens and, on Borough High Street, the John Harvard Library – site of the 19th-century* Marshalsea Prison *(***5***). Walk up Borough High Street, with the library on our right and the* Church of St George the Martyr *(***6***) behind us. Two hundred metres further up, close to the intersection with Southwark Street but still on the right-hand side, is the former yard of* The White Hart *(***7***). Double-back to* The George *(***8***) in the next yard down on the left. Cross the road and cut through* Borough Market *(***9***), veering right to come out on the north side facing the Cathedral. Go left, up Cathedral Street, then right, around the west side of* Southwark Cathedral *(***10***). At the back of the Cathedral, on the other side of the road from the Refectory, we can survey the* River Thames *(***11***). A little further along, where* London Bridge *(***12***) passes above Montague Close, Nancy's Steps are on our left. We climb the steps to survey the river. Downstream of here, in the vicinity of Shad Thames, is* Jacob's Island *(***13***) (for map location see page 54).*

The Dickens!

In the 19th Century, The Borough had some of the most deprived and lawless slums in London, where even policemen feared to tread. This walk visits places connected with Charles Dickens' life and work – both of which were profoundly influenced by his childhood stay here and by this encounter with London's criminal underclass.

Walk begins: *by The Ship inn, Stones End Street (corner of Borough Road and Borough High Street, equidistant from Borough and Elephant and Castle underground stations).* **Ends:** *London Bridge.*

Duration: *short, 30–60 minutes. With optional extension: medium, 60–90 minutes.*

Transport links – Start: *Borough or Elephant and Castle underground station (5 minutes walk).* **Finish:** *London Bridge rail and underground stations.* **Optional extension:** *From Jacob's Island, buses RV1, 188, 381.*

WE BEGIN AT THE SHIP, a pub that was already a century old when the young Dickens lodged nearby. Across the road, just south-east of here, is Newington Gardens, the site of Horsemonger Lane Jail where, in 1849, the famous novelist and campaigner witnessed a public hanging (p 76).

Behind the pub is Stones End Street, site of the **King's Bench (1)** prison, which had moved here from Borough High Street in 1758. The huge prison, built around a rectangular inner yard, extended west from here to the other side of what is now Southwark Bridge Road. In Dickens' novel *Nicholas Nickleby*, Nicholas searches for the Brays' house

> within 'the rules' of the King's Bench Prison […] The Rules were a certain liberty adjoining the prison and comprising some dozen streets in which debtors who could raise money to pay large fees, from which their creditors did not derive any benefit, were permitted to reside.

And in *David Copperfield*, Mr Micawber is imprisoned in the King's Bench for debt. It's a recurring theme in the novels: the effects of debt on the lives of ordinary people, in an age when those unable to support themselves were condemned to the workhouse or the debtors' prison. As we shall shortly see, the author was writing from bitter, first-hand experience.

Walk up to the end of Stones End Street, turn left into Great Suffolk Street, then take the first right, Toulmin Street. Walk up past the Charles Dickens School onto **Lant Street (2)**. Look back. Right on the corner of Lant Street, a blue plaque on the school wall says simply:

> Charles Dickens, 1812–1870, writer, journalist and social reformer.

This seemingly innocuous inscription belies the traumatic circumstances surrounding the 12-year-old Dickens' time in Lant Street. In 1824 his father John Dickens was arrested for debt and thrown in the Marshalsea, one of area's many prisons, on nearby Borough High Street. The precocious, sensitive, middle-class boy from Chatham suddenly found himself cast adrift in south London's criminal underworld:

> the streets around are mean and close: poverty and debauchery lie festering in the crowded alleys.

Nevertheless, he tried to make the best of his new lodgings close to the prison:

> A back attic was found for me at the house of an 'Insolvent-court agent' who lived in Lant Street in the Borough where Bob Sawyer lodged many years afterwards. A bed and bedding were sent over for me and made up on the floor. The little window had a pleasant prospect of a timber yard, and when I took possession of my new abode, I thought it was a Paradise.

Bob Sawyer the Guy's medical student lodges here in *The Pickwick Papers*. Dickens may have taken Bob's surname from the site of the timber yard – Sawyer Street is effectively an extension of Lant Street to the west of Southwark Bridge Road. In the novel, Bob throws a rowdy party, which ends with his

Mint Street Workhouse

landlady throwing out all the guests. As for the other denizens of Lant Street:

> The population is migratory, usually disappearing on the verge of quarter-day and generally by night. His Majesty's revenues are seldom collected in this happy valley, the rents are dubious and the water communication is very frequently cut off.

Crossing Lant Street, we head up Weller Street, one of a number of local streets named after Dickens' characters. Others include Pickwick Street, Quilp Street and Copperfield Street. Dickens thus not only recorded the street life of Victorian Southwark but also helped shape its future identity. At the end of Weller Street we enter Mint Street Park (p 121). This attractive park was the former site of the **Mint Street Workhouse (3)**, said to have been the model for the workhouse in *Oliver Twist*, where Oliver has the nerve to ask for 'more'.

Young Charles was found work in a shoe-blacking factory just north of the river:

> The blacking warehouse […] at old Hungerford Stairs. It was a crazy tumble-down old house, abutting of course on the river, and literally overrun by rats. Its wainscotted rooms, and its rotten floors and stair-case, and the old

grey rats swarming down in the cellars at all times, and the dirt and decay of the place rise up visibly before me, as if I were there again.

There were worse fates than working in Warren's blacking warehouse. In *The Seven Curses of London* (1869), James Greenwood estimated that there were as many as 100,000 destitute children eking out a precarious existence on the streets of London. The dangers they faced were the same as those threatening today's vulnerable street children but in an age with few safeguards or laws to protect them. They were recruited into gangs, made to work as prostitutes, beggars or thieves. The world of *Oliver Twist* – of Nancy, Bill Sikes, Fagin and The Artful Dodger – was a world of Dickens' imagination, but one rooted in grim reality.

This exposure to the life of the underclass would torment Dickens for the rest of his life. Worst of all was the sense of humiliation, the shame at having fallen so far below his station. His novels are rife with capricious reversals of fortune and – something darker, a recurring theme – guilty secrets, pretences, lies. At Warren's blacking factory, Charles was befriended and to some extent protected by an older boy, Bob Fagin, who was himself an orphan:

> No words can express the secret agony of my soul as I sunk into this companionship.

In his autobiographical fragment, Dickens recalls how Bob had walked him home over the river, but how he, ashamed to let his friend see his miserable lodgings, had picked a house at random and, pretending that he lived there, had sent Bob Fagin on his way:

> As a finishing piece of reality in case of his looking back, I knocked at the door, I recollect, and asked, when the woman opened it, if that was Mr Robert Fagin's house.

Did he perhaps resent Bob simply for having known him in such straitened circumstances? Why else should he give his arch villain in *Oliver Twist* – his 'merry old gentlemen', the friend *and* exploiter of homeless children, the evil mastermind behind a school for thieves – the name Fagin?

During his days at the blacking factory, the boy Dickens walked to and from work through **The Mint (4)** – then one of London's most deprived and violent slums (p 27) – just north of where we stand here in Mint Street Park. Twenty years after Dickens' death, Charles Booth's *Survey of Life and Labour of the People in London* still rated Southwark and Bermondsey among the poorest parts of London, with more than half the population living in poverty; here in St Saviour's Parish it was 68%. Booth's 'Descriptive Map of London Poverty' (1889) shows a thin strip of affluence along Borough High Street and other main roads, shaded pink ('fairly comfortable, good ordinary earnings') or even red ('well-to-do middle class'); the back-streets and alleys all around here are shaded blue ('very

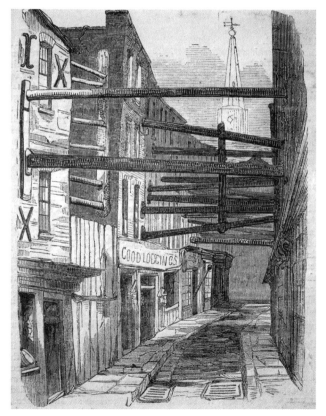

'Mint Street, looking towards High-Street' from *The Builder*, 5 November 1853

poor, casual, chronic want') or black ('lowest class, vicious semi-criminal').

Turning right along the main concourse, we come out of Mint Street Park onto Marshalsea Road, turn right and walk up to the next major junction, crossing to the Church of St George the Martyr. On the north side of the church, just across the road (the short stretch of Tabard Street linking Long Lane with Borough High Street) is St George's Gardens, once the grounds of the **Marshalsea Prison (5)**:

> an oblong pile of barrack building, partitioned into squalid houses standing back to back, so that there were no back rooms; environed by a narrow paved yard, hemmed in by high walls duly spiked at the top.

In 1824, Dickens' father John did time here for his ten-pound debt. With the exception of Charles and his sister Fanny, a boarder at the Royal Academy of Music, the entire Dickens family moved into the prison with him. The novelist drew on this inside knowledge for *Little Dorrit*, in which the child heroine is born and lives with her father in the prison, a true 'child of the Marshalsea'. One night she is actually locked *out* and has to sleep in the adjacent church of **St George the Martyr (6)**, using an old registry as a pillow. In this same church, in happier times, she marries Arthur Clennam. Little Dorrit is depicted in one of the church's stained-glass windows, wearing a poke bonnet. The prison was demolished in the mid-19th Century, and in Dickens' opinion 'the world is none the worse without it'. One of the original walls still stands, enclosing what is now St George's Gardens.

The wall of The Marshalsea

The hapless John Dickens evidently provided the model both for Little Dorrit's father and for Mr Micawber. Charles would never forget his father's last words before being led off to prison, that 'the sun was set upon him for ever'. He would also later vividly recall his own first visit to the Marshalsea:

> My father was waiting for me [...] we went up to his room [...] and cried very much. And he told me, I remember, to take warning by the Marshalsea, and to observe that if a man had twenty pounds a year, and spent nineteen pounds nineteen shillings and sixpence, he would be happy; but that a shilling spent the other way would make him wretched.

The novelist eventually polished up his father's speech for Mr Micawber, who succinctly reveals to David Copperfield this secret of sound economics:

> Annual income twenty pounds, annual expenditure nineteen nineteen six: result happiness. Annual income twenty pounds, annual expenditure twenty pounds ought and six: result misery.

The site of the Marshalsea is now mainly taken by the John Harvard Library, with Southwark's local studies library up the alley between it and the old prison wall. We head north up Borough High Street, with the library on our right and the Church of St George the Martyr behind us. Close to the intersection with Southwark Street, on the right-hand side is the former yard of **The White Hart (7)** (pp 24, 42), where Mr Pickwick meets Sam Weller. Coming back out of the yard, we turn left to walk twenty metres back down Borough High Street to **The George (8)** (pp 24–5). This old coaching-inn and coffee house may also have been the setting for some scenes in *Pickwick Papers*. The George itself is only mentioned once by name – in passing, in *Little Dorrit* – though it certainly fits Dickens' description of the inns of Southwark:

> Great rambling, queer, old places [...] with galleries and staircases, wide enough and antiquated enough to furnish materials for a hundred ghost stories.

Cross the road and cut through **Borough Market (9)** (pp 22–3). The drunken Ben Allen, staggering home from *that party* at Bob Sawyer's gaff in Lant St,

> made the best of his way back, knocked double-knocks at the door of the Borough Market Office and took short naps on the step alternately, until daybreak, under the firm impression that he lived there and had forgotten the key.

The Borough Market Office in question has long since been supplanted. The present office is located to the left of the ornamental gateway to Borough Market. Walk through the market, veering right to come out on the north side, facing the Cathedral. Turn left and follow Cathedral Street up around the west side of the Cathedral. On the corner of Winchester Walk we come upon an attractive late-Victorian building. Inscribed above the door is a date, 1897, and the initials BMT (Borough Market Trustees). This was another Borough Market Office, though it too was in operation only after Dickens' death.

From here, Cathedral Street forks left up to St Mary Overie dock. We go right into Montague Close, around the back of **Southwark Cathedral (10)** (pp 21–2) – or St Saviour's, as it was in Dickens' day. In *The Uncommercial Traveller*, he writes:

> I know the Church of old Gower's tomb (he lies in effigy with his head upon his books) to be the church of St Saviour's, Southwark.

And in a diary entry, dated 2 January 1838, he records a visit to see 'the ruins of the fire in the Borough, thence to the top of Saint Saviour's Church'.

We're now to the north of the Cathedral, between it and the river. The Cathedral's Refectory is to be found in the pleasant courtyard to our right. To our left, an open space between the tall buildings offers a good view of the river. In the opening of *Our Mutual Friend*, Gaffer Hexham and his daughter Lizzie dredge the **River Thames (11)** for the bodies of suicides

> between Southwark Bridge which is of iron and London Bridge which is of stone.

'The Meeting' by George Cruikshank from *Oliver Twist*
by Charles Dickens

At low tide, the young Dickens would have observed hordes of 'mudlarks' scouring the sewage and river mud for rags, bones and other detritus. There was even a price for 'pure', the dog excrement used in the tanning process, which could be sold to Bermondsey tanners for up to ten pence a bucket.

Carry on along Montague Close to where the road runs under the raised approach to **London Bridge (12)**. A plaque on the left marks 'Nancy's Steps', identifying them (incorrectly) as the scene of Nancy's murder in *Oliver Twist*. London Bridge certainly provides the sinister setting for Nancy's meeting with Mr Brownlow and Rose, at which she betrays Fagin's gang in order to save Oliver:

> A mist hung over the river, deepening the red glare of the fires that burnt upon the small craft moored off the different wharfs and rendering darker and more indistinct

the murky buildings on the banks. The old smoke-stained storehouses on either side, rose heavy and dull from the dense mass of roofs and gables, and frowned sternly upon water too black to reflect even their lumbering shapes. The tower of old Saint Saviour's Church, and the spire of Saint Magnus, so long the giant-warders of the ancient bridge, were visible in the gloom.

If we climb the steps to survey the river, even on a misty night, we will see that much has changed, even though the Cathedral tower and spire of St Magnus the Martyr still stand guard on either bank. This is of course a different London Bridge from John Rennie's bridge of 1831, whose 'lower steps widen: so that a person turning the angle of the wall is necessarily unseen by any others on the stairs who chance to be above him, if only a step'. It's there that Noah Claypole lurks, eavesdropping on Nancy to report back to Fagin. So it is true to say that this meeting leads to Nancy's death at the hands of her lover Bill Sikes. But, in the novel, he murders her at his house in Bethnal Green. Sikes' own grisly end takes place downriver, on Jacob's Island.

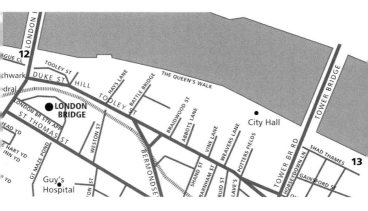

We could extend the walk, crossing the road and going back down the steps by Number 1 London Bridge (p 86), then along the waterfront Queen's Walk, under Tower Bridge and on down Shad Thames to St Saviour's Dock and what was once Jacob's Island (13), the riverside slum so vividly evoked by Dickens:

surrounded by a muddy ditch, six or eight feet deep
and fifteen or twenty feet wide when the tide is in […]
wooden chambers thrusting themselves out above the
mud, and threatening to fall into it – as some have done;
dirt-besmeared walls and decaying foundations; every
repulsive lineament of poverty, every loathsome indication
of filth, rot and garbage; all these ornament the banks
of Folly ditch […] In Jacob's Island, the warehouses are
roofless and empty; the walls are crumbling down; the
windows are windows no more; the doors are falling into
the streets; the chimneys are blackened, but they yield
no smoke.

Or we could linger here on London Bridge, to end on a
lighter note. In the novel that bears his name, David Copperfield
recalls a yet older bridge:

I was wont to sit, in one of the stone recesses watching
the people going by, or to look over the balustrades at
the sun shining in the water and lighting up the golden
flame on top of the Monument.

The Monument, that gold-crowned pillar on the north bank,
can still be seen, though those recesses have long gone, along
with *that* London Bridge, which was demolished in 1831 to
make way for Rennie's. One of the alcoves ended up in Guy's
Hospital (p 116).

An inheritance helped John Dickens to clear his debts and
the family moved back to north London. He had spent roughly
three months in the Marshalsea. Charles's ordeal at Warren's
blacking factory would last less than a year. Yet, out of all
proportion to the short time he spent here, this encounter
with London's dark underbelly would resonate through
Dickens' entire life and work. In a posthumously published
autobiographical fragment, he admits:

My whole nature was so penetrated with the grief and
humiliation of such considerations, that even now, famous
and caressed and happy, I often forget in my dreams that
I have a dear wife and children; even that I am a man;
and wander desolately back to that time in my life.

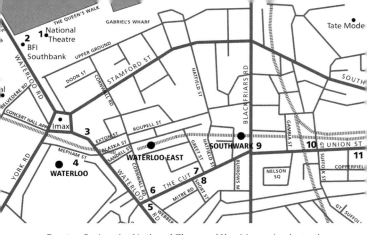

Route: *Facing the National Theatre (**1**) with our backs to the river, turn right and climb the steps up onto Waterloo Bridge (**2**). Turn left and walk south, past the IMAX cinema, crossing Stamford Street. Continue down Waterloo Road, passing the church of St John's Waterloo (**3**) on the left and, just beyond the railway bridge, Waterloo Station (**4**). Carry on down to the next major junction. Cross to the Old Vic (**5**), then turn left and walk to the other end of The Cut (**6**), passing the Young Vic (**7**) on our left and, over the road, the Calder Bookshop (**8**). At the end of The Cut go straight across Blackfriars Road. Number 197, the Palestra Building, stands on the corner, the former site of The Ring (**9**). Continue straight on down Union Street, past the Union Theatre (**10**) on our left and, beyond the crossing with Great Suffolk Street, The Jerwood Space (**11**).*

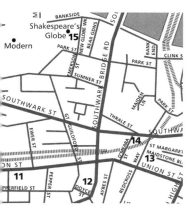

*Walk on for a further 250 metres, past the crossing with Great Guildford Street, until we reach the junction of Union Street with Southwark Bridge Road. Turn right and walk twenty metres down to Playhouse Court at 62 Southwark Bridge Road, the former site of Southwark Playhouse (**12**). Walk back up to the junction with Union Street, turn right, then take the second left up Redcross Way. Go past the gates of Cross Bones Graveyard (**13**), and on under the railway bridge, onto Southwark Street. Twenty metres down on the left is the Menier Theatre (**14**). Rather than turning left, cross Southwark Street and continue up Redcross Way until it meets Park Street. Taking the left branch, go on up towards the river, then turn left again, staying on Park Street. Walk a hundred metres or so further, under Southwark Bridge Road. Take the third turning on the right after the bridge, New Globe Walk, leading up to Shakespeare's Globe (**15**).*

New Theatre Land

The Festival of Britain in 1951 effectively reinvented The South Bank as a citadel of culture. The name 'South Bank' became identified with the arts complex which developed on the riverside around Waterloo Bridge. The National Theatre opened as part of The South Bank in 1976. The Old Vic, just east of Waterloo Station, dates from 1818. This walk visits both theatres, then heads along The Cut beyond the Young Vic into the back-streets further east to take in a world of fringe theatres and site-specific events.

Walk begins: *The National Theatre on The South Bank, Waterloo.* **Ends:** *The Scoop, near Tower Bridge.*

Duration: *long, 90–120 minutes.*

Transport links – Start: *Waterloo underground station, or Embankment station then walk over Waterloo Bridge (5–10 minutes walk).* **Finish:** *bus RV1 from City Hall.*

BACK WHEN ELIZABETHAN THEATRE was flowering on Bankside – and even when Restoration Comedies were being staged in Covent Garden – the area now known as The South Bank was a sparsely inhabited extremity of Lambeth Marsh, bounded by the looping River Thames. People came over the river to visit the water meadows and houses of dubious reputation. In a diary entry of July 1664, Samuel Pepys records his assignation with a 'Mrs Lane' at 'the old house in Lambeth Marsh […] and had my pleasure of her twice'.

During the late 18th Century the commons disappeared, replaced by factories and tenements. Remnants of the old rural Lambeth survived for a time in its public pleasure gardens. With the new urban working class came the circuses and music halls: Astley's Amphitheatre (p 99), The Canterbury Arms and Gatti's Palace of Varieties were all further upstream, in the vicinity of Westminster Bridge. There were also a wide range of theatres – from the Royal Coburg (later renamed the Old Vic) to the penny-gaffs around Lower Marsh and The Cut. In Georgian times, Lambeth Marsh occupied a position somewhat akin to that of the medieval Liberty downstream (p 31), its theatres

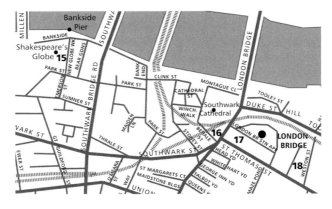

Route (cont.): *From Shakespeare's Globe (15) walk up to the river, then turn right and walk east along Bankside with the river on our left, passing under Southwark Bridge, on past The Anchor, then left under the railway arch to walk down Clink Street. At the end of the street, bear right down Cathedral Street, which becomes Bedale Street, cutting through* **Borough Market (16)**. *Walk to the end of Bedale Street, cross Borough High Street and go down St Thomas Street. On our left is* **The Old Operating Theatre and Herb Garret Museum (17)**. *Walk on to the junction with Weston Street.*

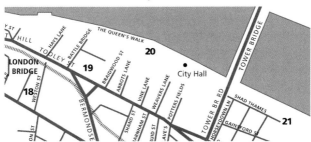

Turn left and walk through the tunnel under the railway arches, passing the original site of **The Drome (18)**, *to Tooley Street. At the end of the tunnel, turn right along Tooley Street, then cross the road to* **The Unicorn (19)**. *Walk further along Tooley Street towards Tower Bridge. Turn left up Weaver's Lane, towards City Hall, the Greater London Authority building on the Queen's Walk. As we face the river, to the left of City Hall is* **The Scoop (20)**, *an open-air auditorium.* **Optional encore:** *walk on under Tower Bridge and continue a few hundred metres along Shad Thames to St Saviour's dock, the old* **Jacob's Island (21)**.

relatively untroubled by the licensing laws and censorship that prevailed north of the river.

The South Bank is a comparatively recent concept, referring to the stretch of the south bank waterfront extending either side of Waterloo Bridge, with its complex of modernist buildings linked by walkways. The Festival of Britain in 1951 transformed the riverside into an enormous exhibition and amusement park. The Festival's legacy was the Royal Festival Hall – just upstream of Waterloo Bridge – around which the South Bank arts centre subsequently developed. The Queen Elizabeth Hall and Hayward Gallery were added in 1968, joined to the Royal Festival Hall by raised walkways. Tucked under the arches of Waterloo Bridge, BFI Southbank (formerly the 'National Film Theatre') had its origins in the Telecinema which featured in the Festival of Britain.

The **National Theatre (1)** opened in 1976. Its uncompromising modernist design by Denys Lasdun excited much controversy; Prince Charles later described it as 'a way of building a nuclear power station in the middle of London without anyone objecting'. The building comprises three theatres: the Olivier, the Lyttelton and the Cottesloe. Tales abound of cast members getting lost backstage in the labyrinth of corridors. One wouldn't expect such an unashamedly functional modern theatre to have acquired the mythologies that attach themselves to older, more gothic establishments. Yet

The National Theatre, South Bank

it was here, in 1989, that Daniel Day-Lewis, playing Hamlet, had to leave the stage mid-performance, having apparently seen his own father's ghost.

As a company, the National Theatre dates back to 1963, when it was based at the Old Vic. Laurence Olivier, its founding Artistic Director, was succeeded by Peter Hall, who oversaw the move to this purpose-built home on the South Bank. In 1988 the word 'Royal' was added to the name, much against the wishes of Hall's successor Richard Eyre. The 'Royal' has since been quietly dropped. Notable in-house productions of the 80s included Howard Brenton's *The Romans In Britain* – which provoked Mary Whitehouse to bring a private prosecution for obscenity against director Michael Bogdanov, although she hadn't even seen the play – and Tony Harrison's *The Mysteries*. There were also guest productions, including Ken Campbell's adaptation of the *Illuminatus!* trilogy.

Richard Eyre expanded the range of visiting companies to include Theatre de Complicite and Robert Lepage. During Eyre's tenure, Declan Donnellan directed *Angels in America,* Stephen Daldry staged a hugely successful revival of *An Inspector Calls,* and Eyre himself directed Ian McKellen in *Richard III.* He was succeeded by Trevor Nunn, oft criticised for concentrating too much on musicals with one eye on a West End transfer. Under Nicholas Hytner's stewardship, the National's productions included *His Dark Materials*, *The History Boys* and *Jerry Springer – the Opera*. In summer there are open-air performances in the forecourt known as Theatre Square.

Climb the steps to **Waterloo Bridge (2)**. From here we can view the various theatres, galleries and concert halls that loosely comprise the South Bank arts complex laid out on either side of the bridge. Gazing upriver, beyond the Royal Festival Hall, we can see the London Eye, a giant modern version of the Ferris wheel that once graced the Festival of Britain. Just beyond that is the former County Hall with the Houses of Parliament across the river. In the 1980s, during the last days of the Greater London Council (GLC), huge banners were hung on County Hall expressing opposition to the policies of the Thatcher Government: a latter-day reiteration of the south bank's ancient autonomy and traditions of radical dissent.

Walk south, heading away from the river down Waterloo Road, passing the IMAX cinema with its giant (26 x 20m) screen. This was formerly the site of Cuper's (or 'Cupid's') Garden, a disreputable pleasure garden which closed in 1760. By the 1980s the sunken bull-ring in which the IMAX now stands had become the heart of a cardboard city for the homeless that snaked out around the nearby railway arches and subways.

Follow the road across Stamford Street and on down Waterloo Road, braving the noise, the traffic and what some guidebooks refer to as 'undesirables'. **St John's Waterloo (3)**, the church on our left, offers refuge to homeless people and those who might otherwise slip through the net of social care. It opened in 1824, one of several 'Waterloo churches' built to commemorate the victory over Napoleon at the Battle of Waterloo.

Go on under the bridge, with **Waterloo Station (4)** on our right. By the time the station opened in 1848, the surrounding area had become one of the poorest parts of London. The massive population increase, compounded by a cholera epidemic, meant that all the local cemeteries were soon filled to capacity. From 1870, the London Necropolis Railway began ferrying the dead from Waterloo to the Necropolis Cemetery at Brookwood, near Woking. This original Necropolis station was demolished in 1900 to make way for the expansion of the main station. It was replaced by a purpose-built London Necropolis Station on Westminster Bridge Road, which carried on transporting corpses for another half-century.

Waterloo Bridge had opened in 1817, boosting the fortunes of the surrounding 'penny-gaff' theatres, music halls and other lowbrow entertainments; theatrical digs proliferated as the slums were colonised by actors and 'artistes'. During the First World War, many troops passed through Waterloo Station on their way to the front, often staying at the United Services Club (now the Union Jack Club in Sandell Street, off to the left). The ranks of jobbing actors were swelled by footloose soldiers looking for a good night out. Between the wars, Waterloo Road became a remarkably inclusive *demi-monde* where straight working-class men consorted with theatrical 'queens' and prostitutes of both sexes.

Stay on the left-hand side and carry on down to the next major junction. Across the road is the **Old Vic (5)**. It opened in 1818 as the Royal Coburg Theatre, taking its name from its royal patrons, Princess Charlotte and her husband Prince Leopold of Saxe-Coburg. Like other south London theatres it staged popular melodramas. The distinguished actor Edmund Kean tried to bring Shakespeare to the masses, playing Lear, Macbeth, Richard III and Othello in the space of a week. One night, taking his curtain call, Kean told the rowdy audience: 'I have never acted to such a set of ignorant, unmitigated brutes as I see before me.'

In 1833, the Royal Coburg was renamed in honour of Princess (soon to be Queen) Victoria, and became popularly known as 'the Old Vic'. The social reformer Emma Cons acquired the theatre in 1880, renaming it the Royal Victoria Coffee Hall. In an attempt to improve its dubious reputation, she banned the sale of alcohol and the performing of Shakespeare, which was considered too stimulating for polite society. In 1912,

Cons' niece Lilian Baylis took over the running of the theatre; her ballet company, directed by Ninette de Valois, performed here before moving to Sadler's Wells. During the First World War, Baylis famously refused to stop the show even during air-raids.

Baylis soon reinstated Shakespeare's plays in the Old Vic repertoire. During the early 1920s, the company produced all the plays in the First Folio. In 1929 John Gielgud played Hamlet; that same year he founded the Old Vic Company. Over the next five or so years, he was joined by Ralph Richardson, Peggy Ashcroft, Alec Guinness and Laurence Olivier.

The Old Vic, stage door

When the Old Vic company disbanded in 1963, Olivier became director of the new National Theatre Company, working with young actors like Anthony Hopkins and Maggie Smith. Its first production was *Hamlet* with Peter O'Toole as the Prince. Despite 'House Full' signs at every performance, the company made a loss on its first season. In 1964, the National produced its first world première, *The Royal Hunt of the Sun* by Peter Shaffer. Ted Hughes' adaptation of Seneca's *Oedipus* was directed by Peter Brook, known for his unconventional approach to rehearsals. For one exercise, each actor was asked to step forward and tell the company what most frightened them. When John Gielgud's turn came, he replied simply: 'We open on Tuesday.' Gielgud survived the experience and went on to co-star with Ralph Richardson in Harold Pinter's *No Man's Land* directed by Peter Hall. This was one of the National Theatre's last productions at the Old Vic before it left in 1976 for its new home on the South Bank.

Six years later, the Old Vic theatre was bought and restored by the Canadian businessman Ed Mirvish. By the 90s it was enjoying something of a revival. In 2003 Kevin Spacey, having already performed at the Old Vic when *The Iceman Cometh* transferred from the Almeida Theatre in north London, became the first artistic director of the (new) Old Vic Theatre Company.

Turn left down **The Cut (6)**. Along with Lower and Upper Marsh – now behind us, on the other side of the Waterloo Road – The Cut was the home of the penny-gaffs, makeshift theatres in dilapidated buildings where the public paid one or two pence to watch melodramas or racy excerpts from Shakespeare. Back in 1859, George Sala described the 'New Cut' as 'sordid, squalid and [...] disreputable'. The street has recently acquired shiny new developments and upmarket restaurants, yet retains something of its old seedy charm. On our right is the renovated National Theatre Studio, primarily used for the development of new work.

Further down on the left is the **Young Vic (7)**, established by Frank Dunlop in 1970 to present experimental work to a young audience. The design of the Young Vic encouraged this kind of radical approach, its thrust stage and intimate seating creating a highly charged theatre space. The original breeze-block shack, erected on a bomb-site and incorporating one of the surviving houses, was only intended for short-term use, yet somehow lasted into the next millennium. When the theatre finally had to close for rebuilding, the Company kept going, performing in more than forty venues. In October 2006, the refurbished, redesigned Young Vic Theatre reopened.

Just across the road: the **Calder Bookshop (8)**. During the 1950s and 60s John Calder published Nobel Prize-winning writers, including Samuel Beckett, alongside banned authors such as Henry Miller and William Burroughs. Short plays and readings from Beckett, Joyce and other influential writers were presented here at the Bookshop Theatre, 51 The Cut.

Walk on to the end of The Cut and cross Blackfriars Road to Number 197 – the Palestra Building – designed by Will Alsop. Before its predecessor, Orbit House, was demolished, an exhibition was held. Artists carved the faces of Marx, Lenin,

Che Guevara and other socialist icons on the floor-boards. The exhibition also featured old photos of The Ring, where boxing matches were staged on this site from 1910 until 1940.

The Ring (9) was the brainchild of Bella Burge, a music hall entertainer, and her husband Dick, a former boxer. Bella had been more or less adopted by Marie Lloyd's family (p 103), appearing as one of the Sisters Lloyd before becoming Marie's dresser. She met Dick Burge when they appeared on the same bill at Gatti's music hall. Within a month of their marriage in 1901, Dick was imprisoned for fraud. Even Marie felt obliged to distance herself from her old friend for a time.

Boxing was a popular sport among the south London working class: Bermondsey, a couple of kilometres to the east, had produced a succession of British champions. When Dick Burges was released from prison in 1909, he and Bella set about establishing a boxing ring. They leased the derelict Surrey Chapel that used to stand here on Blackfriars Road.

Built in 1783 for the charismatic preacher Rowland Hill, the chapel's main hall was circular in shape, allowing 'no place for the devil to hide'. After Hill's death, the chapel had continued to be used until 1876, when it had been converted into a factory. In the months leading up to the opening of The Ring in 1910, Bella employed local tramps to help renovate the (by then) dilapidated building. She operated a soup kitchen in a back room, where Marie Lloyd sometimes helped out and gave impromptu performances. The Ring was the first boxing hall to admit women, led of course by Bella. It brought a measure of respectability to boxing – it was visited by film stars, such as Marlene Dietrich, and even by the Prince of Wales – but by the Second World War its fortunes were in decline. In 1940 it was effectively demolished by an enemy bomb.

Charles Dickens remembered the chapel from his walk home to Lant Street from his work in the blacking factory near Hungerford Steps (pp 47–9):

> My usual way home was over Blackfriars Bridge and down that turning in Blackfriars Road which has Rowland Hill's Chapel on one side and the likeness of a golden dog licking a golden pot over a shop door on the other.

The Union Theatre gate

Cross the road and follow in Dickens' footsteps along Union Street, where new developments uneasily coexist with what's left of the old working-class neighbourhoods. Here we leave behind those great citadels of culture, venturing into a world of fringe theatres and experimental site-specific performances. On the left, Number 204, tucked in under the railway arches, is the **Union Theatre (10)**. The venue was established in 1998 by Sasha Regan, who converted the arches with the help of friends and family. Like many small theatres, it is committed to supporting new work. Cross Great Suffolk Street. A little further along Union Street, on the right, a former school has been refurbished as the **Jerwood Space (11)**, with art galleries and rehearsal rooms for theatre companies.

We walk on a further 250 metres, past the crossing with Great Guildford Street, until we reach the junction of Union Street with the much larger Southwark Bridge Road. Hang a right and walk twenty metres down to Playhouse Court at Number 62 Southwark Bridge Road. Founded in 1993 by Juliet Alderdice and Tom Wilson, **Southwark Playhouse (12)** survived here for thirteen years, mixing in-house productions with new work from visiting companies. The theatre, with its flexible seating, lent itself to productions which incorporated the building into their sets: a character in a doss-house scene might draw open a ragged curtain to reveal the legs of the passers-by in Southwark Bridge Road. *The Halloween of Cross Bones*, a ritual drama performed on the 31 October each year (pp 80–1), was first performed at Southwark Playhouse in 1998, ending with a procession to the nearby graveyard. The Playhouse's educational projects were well respected throughout The Borough. In 2006 they staged a promenade performance of *The Canterbury Tales,* beginning at The George inn on Borough High Street and visiting various sites in the locality. At the end of that year, the landlord requested the premises for his own use; the company relocated to the railway arches under London Bridge.

Walk back up to the junction with Union Street, turn right, then second left up Redcross Way. Go past the shrine on our right at the gates of **Cross Bones Graveyard (13)** (pp 28–9, 120–1), itself a site of unlicensed public performances, especially at Halloween when crowds fill the street for the annual *Halloween of Cross Bones* celebration. Go on under the railway bridge and then up onto Southwark Street. Twenty metres down on the left is the **Menier Theatre (14)**, which opened in 2003 in a converted 1870s chocolate factory. Most of the original timber beams and ironwork have been preserved and restored. The building also features a gallery, restaurant and rehearsal room.

Instead of turning left, though, cross Southwark Street and continue up Redcross Way until it meets Park Street. Taking the left branch, go on up towards the river and then, again, take the Park Street turning to the left. Walk west, past the original sites of The Globe and The Rose (pp 36–8). The third turning on the right after the bridge is New Globe Walk, leading up to **Shakespeare's Globe (15)**, which is best viewed

The Menier Theatre in the Chocolate Factory

from the Bankside river-front. Often dismissed as a tourist attraction, this reconstructed Elizabethan playhouse by the river (p 33) can claim to have revitalised the playing of Shakespeare and his contemporaries. Its first Artistic Director, Mark Rylance, balanced an intensely personal response to Shakespeare with the perceived need to popularise the plays. The reinstatement of 'groundlings' – audience members standing in the pit around the stage – engendered a sense of complicity between actor and audience. Shakespeare's Globe has also commissioned new writing and sometimes hosts visiting companies.

My own cycle of contemporary Mystery Plays, *The Southwark Mysteries*, had its première here on Easter Sunday – also St George's Day and 'Shakespeare's birthday' – on 23 April 2000. This epic community drama climaxed at The Globe with Christ's death. The audience was then led along Bankside by a band of devils playing jazz – 'the Devil's music' – to Southwark Cathedral, where they found Satan holding forth from the pulpit. The Great Accuser's claim on the lost souls of Southwark was frustrated by the coming of Christ to 'harrow Hell'.

Facing the Globe with the river behind us, turn left and walk along Bankside, keeping the river on our left, passing under Southwark Bridge, with its Frost Fair engraving, and on past The Anchor. Now turn left under the railway arch along Clink Street. At the end of the street, bear right down Cathedral Street, which becomes Bedale Street, cutting through Borough Market.

This is the route taken by The Lion's Part on their colourful processions from The Globe to **Borough Market (16)** (pp 22–3). The Lion's Part is a troupe of actors who regularly perform on Bankside to mark traditional English seasonal festivals. Their October Plenty event, held in the market on the last Sunday in October, features the performance of a play, an 'execution of John Barleycorn' and the dismembering of a giant 'Corn Queene' effigy; the fruits and vegetables tied to her wicker frame are torn off and thrown to the audience. The event traditionally ends with The Green Man (Berry Man) leading a procession down to Cross Bones Graveyard. Once there, an actress playing Ceres, the Roman goddess of corn, leads the crowd in tying corn crosses and fertility symbols to the shrine at the gates. Borough Market has been the venue for other theatre and music events; in October 2006 it staged its own 250th anniversary celebration.

Cutting through Borough Market, walk to the end of Bedale Street, cross Borough High Street and go down St Thomas Street. Groups like The Lion's Part, rather than being tied to a specific theatre, specialise in performing in public spaces. Similarly, the London Bubble, based a couple of kilometres downriver in Rotherhithe, present their pantomimes and promenade performances in tents or in the open air.

In this immediate vicinity, churches, pubs, warehouses and railway arches have hosted a huge range of site-specific performances. **The Old Operating Theatre (17)** (pp 117–8), number 9a St Thomas Street, is an original and perfectly preserved 19th-century operating theatre. Medical students once packed the raked amphitheatre, jostling to watch surgeons perform operations without anaesthetics. The theatre hasn't changed, though these days it features performance poetry alongside suitably gory lectures on the history of medicine.

Continue walking east along St Thomas Street, with the Victorian brick arches of London Bridge Station on our left. The arches and caverns under this railway viaduct have been commandeered for an astonishing range of performances. The SHUNT collective animated their tunnels with feathered showgirls.

Carry on past Stainer Street (Dean Street as was, when John Keats was writing his poems there), to the next tunnel on the left, at the junction with Weston Street. Don't be put off by the fumes – it *is* a road tunnel, but at least there's a pavement!

Turn left up Weston Street and walk north from St Thomas Street through the tunnel leading to Tooley Street. All the caverns on our left are now part of SeOne, one of London's biggest dance clubs, with a capacity of 3000. The venue's reputation was made in 1999, when it was known as **The Drome (18)**, home to the legendary *Warp* parties. These 24-hour parties were built around a revival of Neil Oram's 24-hour play, *The Warp,* performed non-stop in one of the caverns, with six others housing multimedia performances, dance floors, a gallery, a chill, a healing space and a 'Tantric Goddess Temple' equipped with a hot tub that could hold up to fifty naked ravers. It couldn't last, and closed in 2000 when an application to renew its licence was refused.

The new SeOne owners sand-blasted the blackened brick walls and cleaned up their Health-and-Safety act. These days the parties are strictly legal.

At the end of the tunnel, go right, along Tooley Street, then cross the road to **The Unicorn (19)** – the children's theatre at Number 147. The original Unicorn Theatre grew out of a Mobile Theatre founded by Caryl Jenner in 1947. The company toured in buses bringing children's theatre to out-of-the-way places. Twenty years on, they obtained a lease on the Arts Theatre in the West End. Plans for a purpose-built theatre in Southwark go back to the 70s – the proposed site was then at Blackfriars Bridge. In 2001, the project received Arts Council support with Lottery Funding of £4.5 million. The new theatre opened in 2005. During its first year the company performed to more than 70,000 people.

Walk further along Tooley Street towards Tower Bridge. Here, at the end of Weaver's Lane, on the Queen's Walk, is City Hall, the Greater London Authority building. Between here and More London Place is **The Scoop (20)**, an open-air auditorium. If there isn't a performance in progress you may have to ask or intuit where it is; if something's on, you'll see it. Will this free theatre become mere animation, cultural window-dressing for More London's new commercial development? First signs, at least, were encouraging: a production of Brecht's *The Caucasian Chalk Circle* showed a willingness to engage and challenge its peripatetic audience.

Optional encore

If we've got the energy, we could stroll on under Tower Bridge and along Shad Thames to St Saviour's Dock, the location of the once notorious **Jacob's Island (21)**, where Bill Sikes is cornered and killed in *Oliver Twist*. There are, so far as I know, no theatres in the immediate vicinity, but the refurbished wharves and warehouses, some linked by gantries at the upper level, could be straight out of a film-set – and indeed this was the location for a scene from *A Fish Called Wanda*. The smell of the tidal dock may yet carry a trace of the stench that once hung over 'Folly Ditch' (pp 54–5).

Route: *From the* Elephant and Castle (**1**) *walk up Newington Causeway to* The Ship (**2**). *We then retrace our steps to the zebra crossing, cross Newington Causeway and continue down Avonmouth Street into Newington Gardens, the old site of the* Horsemonger Lane Jail (**3**). *Come out of the north gate onto Harper Road. Walk up Brockham Street, then left through* Trinity Church Square (**4**). *Turn right to walk east down Trinity Street. Take the first left, Globe Street, and walk up to the junction with Great Dover Street. To the right is the site of a* Romano-British cemetery (**5**). *Cross Great Dover Street and walk up Pilgrimage Street to* Becket House (**6**) *on the corner with Tabard Street. Facing Becket House, turn right and walk north-west up Tabard Street, past the site of a* Roman Temple (**7**) *to our right, then cross Long Lane, passing the* Church of St George the Martyr (**8**) *on our left. Turn right up Borough High Street and right again up Angel Place, the alley running alongside the John Harvard Library, to see a surviving wall of the former* Marshalsea Prison (**9**). *Walk back onto Borough High Street. Cross the road, looking back at the old façade of* The Crown (**10**). *Go west along Marshalsea Road, then turn right up Redcross Way. Go straight across at the crossroads with Union Street. On the right is the site of the* Cross Bones Graveyard (**11**) *(for map location see overleaf).*

The Ghost Walk

Magic and mystery on a walk from Elephant and Castle to London Bridge – haunted pubs and music halls; a Borough magician and a female gladiator; the outcast dead of Cross Bones Graveyard, the legend of Mary Overie and the spookiest stretch of the River Thames. This walk, though it may be taken by day, is best taken at night.

Walk begins: *Elephant and Castle, Bakerloo Line tube station, corner of Newington Causeway.* **Ends:** *Olaf Stairs, on the Queen's Walk riverside near London Bridge.*

Duration: *long, 90–120 minutes.*

Transport links – Start: *Elephant and Castle underground and rail stations.* **Finish:** *London Bridge underground and rail stations.*

THE ELEPHANT AND CASTLE (1) may seem an unlikely place to embark on a ghost-hunt. Yet here, deep within the tunnels of the Bakerloo Line Underground Station, even after they've closed the station for the night, staff report hearing footsteps. When they go to investigate, the platforms are deserted.

Behind the station, on a site now occupied by the South Bank University, stood the South London Palace of Varieties (1860–1955) (pp 102–3), one of the great Victorian music halls. Built on the site of an 1840s Roman Catholic chapel, the South London Palace was widely believed to be haunted by nuns. There was a mirror in the back of the auditorium in which the actors could see themselves on stage. It was claimed that, once a year, the mirror clouded over, then cleared and lit up with the images of three crucifixes. Several men tried to remove the mirror. All were said to have died in suspicious circumstances.

The artist and occultist Austin Osman Spare had his studio at 56a Walworth Road; it was bombed during the Blitz, along with most of the other buildings on what was to become the Elephant and Castle south roundabout. Spare then lodged in a hostel at 86 Walworth Road. His last years were spent in Brixton but, until his death in 1956, he never lost his connection with The Borough[1].

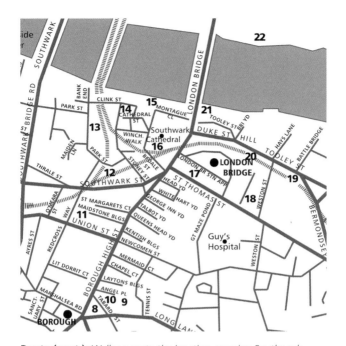

Route (cont.): *Walk on up to the junction, crossing Southwark Street, then straight on up Redcross Way. Turn right at the junction with* Park Street (**12**), *walking a short distance up the street, then retrace our steps, this time following Park Street around to the right. Walk up towards the river, through the district once known as* Deadman's Place (**13**). *Just before The Anchor, turn right and walk under the railway arch down Clink Street. Walk to the far end, beyond* Winchester Palace (**14**), *then bear left to* St Mary Overie dock (**15**). *Coming back from the river-front, bear left around the Cathedral, passing* Green Dragon Court (**16**), *turn left down Bedale Street, coming out on Borough High Street. Cross Borough High Street and walk down St Thomas Street. On our left is* The Old Operating Theatre and Herb Garret Museum (**17**). *Walk on down St Thomas Street with the railway arch on our left. At the junction with Weston Street turn left and walk through the tunnel to Tooley Street, passing the site of* The Drome (**18**). *Emerging onto Tooley Street, to our right is the* Britain At War exhibition (**19**). *Turn left, walking up past* The London Dungeon (**20**) *to the Joiner Street entrance to London Bridge rail and underground stations. Here we cross Tooley Street and walk straight over to Olaf House. Go through the alley, Olaf Stairs, to view the Thames from the Queen's Walk. To our left is* London Bridge (**21**) *and, on the north bank, the* Church of St Magnus the Martyr (**22**). *To our right, on the far bank near Tower Bridge, is the* Tower of London (**23**) *(for map location see opposite).*

In 1904, having exhibited at the Royal Academy aged 17, Spare had been hailed as 'A Young London Genius'. However, he soon fell out with the art establishment, pursuing his own eccentric course. Shunning the galleries, he exhibited in his flat and at local pubs, selling his paintings to locals for two or three guineas. A photograph from the *South London Press* – dated 4 November 1949 – shows the interior of the Temple Bar, Walworth Road: Barmaid Pam holds one of Spare's paintings; a bunch of locals stare at it, faintly bemused, as the artist – 'foot on the bar rail' – explains his exhibition. This exhibition at the Temple Bar in 1949 featured

> new studies in psycho-physiognomy by realism, dual-perspective, automatism and other diverse means of rhythm and reorientation – relating to Southwark Types.

Spare employed automatic writing and drawing to reveal the spirit world; he also painted realistic portraits and nudes. His life-models included local shop-girls and many elderly people, including a 93-year-old woman. These days his works are exhibited in prestigious galleries and are much prized among collectors. The Temple Bar is still there on the Walworth Road, less than a kilometre south of here – but we're going to head north, up Newington Causeway, the old Roman causeway that carried Stane Street over the marshes and north to London Bridge. Along the way, we'll renew our acquaintance with Austin Osman Spare, the Borough magician. But first…

Staying on the left-hand side of the road, walk up Newington Causeway. Pass under the railway bridge. A hundred metres north, where Newington Causeway turns into Borough High Street at the junction with Borough Road, is **The Ship (2)** –

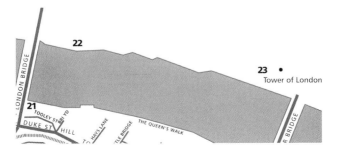

(allegedly) one of The Borough's most haunted pubs. There was the lady in period dress who vanished into thin air; the spooky child's voice calling the bar-staff by name. There are ongoing reports of poltergeist activity: barrel-wedges tampered with; cellar-taps inexplicably turned off. One barmaid reportedly saw a bony hand in a black cloak. The pub, built in 1716, was used as a court-house before the Surrey County Sessions was built across the road. That bony hand, could it once have belonged to a hanging judge?

We're outside the pub, at the junction of Borough Road with the south end of Borough High Street. Looking left, a hundred and fifty metres north, we can see the spectral bone-white spire of the Church of St George the Martyr.

First, though, we go back across Borough Road and retrace our steps down Newington Causeway. Cross the road at the next zebra crossing, then take the first left down Avonmouth Street and through Newington Gardens – still known locally as Jail Gardens in memory of the **Horsemonger Lane Jail (3)** which stood here from 1791 to 1879. It was here, on 13 November 1849, that Dickens (pp 45–55) witnessed the public hanging of Maria Manning and her husband, for poisoning their lodger (her ex-lover) in Weston Street, Bermondsey. In the 19th Century, public executions were regarded as a form of entertainment. On a silent, moonless night, we may still hear the creak of the gallows, the strangled death-cries of the victims, the moan of the crowd…

Follow the main path around to the left through Newington Gardens to come out of the north gate onto Harper Road at the corner of Brockham Street. Walk up Brockham Street, then left through Trinity Church Square to Trinity Street, then go right and stop at the north-east corner of the churchyard. From here, there's a fine view of **Trinity Church (4)** – now the Henry Wood Hall, used chiefly for orchestra rehearsals. The church was built in 1824; work on the square commenced the year after. The statue in the churchyard is believed to date back to the 15th Century and to have once adorned Westminster Hall. Local children report that if you run along the railings in front of the church the head of the statue follows you. A trick of the eye? Or do these wise children know something we don't? Try it, why don't we? Crouch down to child-size, run along the railings and see the head move!

With the church on our right, we walk east down Trinity Street. Take the first left, Globe Street, and walk the short distance up to the junction with Great Dover Street. Over the road, about fifty metres away to our right – next to Number 165, the red-brick building – was the site of a **Romano-British cemetery (5)** located just off the former Watling Street. Here archaeologists found a Roman terracotta oil-lamp in the shape of a legionnaire's sandal. In 1996, they discovered the mortal remains of the so-called 'female gladiator': her pelvic bone and the seeds of exotic fruits from a graveside feast, dating from the 1st or 2nd Century. Even though she had been buried with honour, her grave lay outside the walls of the cemetery. The strongest clues as to her identity were a number of decorated lamps found in her grave: one bore the image of a gladiator; three others depicted Anubis, the jackal-headed Egyptian guide of the dead. The Romans identified Anubis with Mercury, the god of fallen gladiators. They also believed that a gladiator's blood was endowed with aphrodisiac and healing powers. Female gladiators were outlawed by the Emperor Septimus Severus in 200 AD.

Cross Great Dover Street and walk up Pilgrimage Street to Tabard Gardens, a long rectangular park surrounded by the Tabard Gardens Estate, an example of early 20th-century social housing. During the 1920s, number **52 Becket House (6)** on the Tabard Gardens Estate was home to Austin Osman Spare, the artist we encountered earlier, the chaos magician regarded by his disciples as the 'True Master of the Left-hand Path'.

Spare practised an idiosyncratic magic, using graphic symbols or 'sigils' to activate his subconscious. His writings include *The Book of Pleasure* and a grimoire: *The Living Word of Zos*. Spare's

'The Death Posture: Second Position' by Austin Osman Spare

esoteric techniques are not for the faint-hearted – he employed what he termed 'The Death Posture' to induce altered states of consciousness. He also claimed to be able to materialise his thoughts. When tested by the Society for Psychical Research he is said to have succeeded not only in reading his examiner's mind, but in materialising what was in it – a pair of slippers!

Facing Becket House, we turn right and walk north-west up Tabard Street towards the church of St George the Martyr. To our right is Tabard Square, a recent high-rise development crowned with a giant barometric light-box, which changes colour according to changes in air-pressure. During its construction, on-site excavations* uncovered the site of a **Roman Temple (7)** with the first known inscription refer-ring to 'Londiniensium […] This dedication to the spirits of the Emperors and the god Mars Camulus was set up by Tiberinius Celerianus'. Tiberinius was a trade negotiator to London, a citizen of the Bellovaci tribe in north-east France. Given Austin Osman Spare's apparent psychic powers, might he have intuited that his humble council flat lay directly between a temple and a cemetery?

Carry on up Tabard Street, crossing Long Lane. To our left is the **Church of St George The Martyr (8)** (p 50), with the white spire we saw earlier (looking up from The Ship). The present St George's was built in 1734, though there's been a church here at the crossroads since at least the 12th Century. Extensive repair work in 2005 involved underpinning the foundations to stop the church sinking into the marshy ground. A number of coffins were removed from the crypt. Back in 1938, a previous work of restoration had uncovered 'masses of skulls and bones', reputedly causing workers to down tools in the fear of catching the plague. One of the church bells once hung in Horsemonger Lane Jail; it used to toll the death-knell for convicted criminals.

By day, we can enter the gate on our right, crossing St George's Gardens to view the surviving wall of the **Marshalsea Prison (9)** (p 50). Better still, in the dead of night, go on to

---

*   From the 1990s, extensive archaeological excavations in The Borough have uncovered important Roman remains, challenging the accepted view that Southwark was at that time a mere outpost of The City. A dig prior to work on the Jubilee Line Extension unearthed a Roman arcade in the vicinity of London Bridge Station. The 'Londiniensium' inscription implies that Southwark is at least as old as The City itself.

the end of Tabard Street, turn right into Borough High Street, then right again to walk half-way up Angel Place, the alley that runs alongside the John Harvard Library. With our backs to the Local Studies Library, facing that same Marshalsea prison wall, we do indeed 'stand among the crowding ghosts of many miserable years.' (Dickens, preface to *Little Dorrit*, 1857)

The Church of St George the Martyr

Walk back down the alley to Borough High Street. Cross the road, pausing to look back at the old façade of a renovated building, adorned with plaster crowns, between the library and the church. This was once **The Crown (10)**, the public house where, in 1902, George Chapman poisoned his wife. He was arrested and hanged at Wandsworth prison. Not long after, the pub staff reported hearing phantom footsteps. The licensee's mother saw a man walking up the stairs and then vanishing. Then there was the sound of a child crying that seemed to come from behind a wall. The landlord investigated further and discovered four rooms that had been boarded up. In one of them was a child's cot. The landlord threw it away, whereupon the ghostly crying immediately stopped. The pub was demolished in the 1970s, though the original façade was preserved.

Go west along Marshalsea Road, then turn right into Redcross Way. Walk a couple of hundred metres up the long straight road towards the distant railway arch. Go straight across at the crossroads with Union Street. A little further up, on the right, is an iron gate adorned with ribbons, flowers and totemic offerings. Through the gates we can see a plot of vacant land, some of which is used as a works depot. The south part of the site (to our right as we look in through the gates) has been fenced off – a wild garden has taken hold there.

Back in 1996, researching the history of the site in the local studies library, I came across the following entry in *The Annals of St Mary Overie* (1833):

> The women [...] are said not to have been allowed Christian burial unless reconciled to the church before their death and there is an unconsecrated burial ground known as Cross Bones at the corner of Redcross Street, formerly called the Single Woman's burial ground, which is said to have been used for this purpose.

The archivist goes on to quote Walter Scott:

> A place of burial, for such dead
> As having died in mortal sin
> Might not be laid the church within.

I soon established the location of the site, to find it had recently been excavated by Museum of London archaeologists prior to being dug up during work on the Jubilee Line Extension!*

And here we are, at the **Cross Bones Graveyard (11)** (pp 28–9, 120–1). On 31 October 1998 the first *Halloween of Cross Bones*, a contemporary ritual drama, was conducted in Southwark Playhouse (pp 66–7) on Southwark Bridge Road, a few minutes west of here. The performance turned into a candlelit procession from the theatre to the graveyard. A memorial plaque, made by a local working girl, was fixed to a wall; ribbons and mementoes tied to the gates to make a shrine. That same week – a stroke of synchronicity – the Museum of London opened its exhibition of *London Bodies*, featuring 'a young woman's syphilitic skull from Redcross Way, Southwark'. The museum had removed 148 skeletons from the Cross Bones site; by their estimate this represented 1% of the total burials.

---

* In *The Southwark Mysteries* by John Constable, the trickster John Crow encounters the spirit of The Goose, a medieval prostitute who claims that her bones were unearthed during the excavations at Cross Bones. The Goose reveals her 'secret history' in poems, songs and mystery plays. Since 1998, these works have been performed at many places around The Borough and Bankside – including Shakespeare's Globe, Southwark Cathedral, The Old Operating Theatre, The Drome and at the Cross Bones site.

Bronze plaque on the gates of Cross Bones Graveyard

The Halloween of Cross Bones has been celebrated every year since as a local seasonal festival, where people from many walks of life come to honour those who were once shut out of society.

In 2006, the London Borough of Southwark installed planters with ivy to frame the gates, with an official plaque identifying the site as an ancient burial ground for prostitutes and paupers. The bronze plaque bears the image of a rampant goose and the epitaph:

The Outcast Dead
R.I.P.

With the graveyard on our right, walk on up to the junction, crossing Southwark Street, then straight on up Redcross Way. Turn right at the junction with **Park Street (12)**, a place so atmospheric that it regularly features in films. Madonna filmed a music video here. Observe the green painted warehouse tucked in on the right, with the graffiti: 'This is not a photo-opportunity.' BANKSYesque. Not so long ago, guerrilla ghost-artist BANKSY was all over The Borough. His giant mural 'Chequebook Vandalism' – depicting an invasion of bowler-hatted, umbrella-wielding developers – was stencilled onto the Clink Street railway arch. (It'd be worth a fortune now, if only the council hadn't had it painted over.) BANKSY cheekily took out the 'DE' of 'BANKSIDE' adding a ' \ ' to the 'I' to spell out his *nom de guerre*. BANKSY, or an imitator, even tagged the

Banksy was here? The 'Chequebook Vandalism' mural in Clink Street

wooden fence around Cross Bones with a goose and the legend: 'Whither do you wander?'

Wanderer, lift up your gaze: that's the tower of Southwark Cathedral – perfectly framed at the end of Park Street, sunlit by day, spectral by night – a pilgrim's vision. Now retrace your steps back to the junction with Redcross Way, following the curve of Park Street round to the right, and walk up to Bank End by the river, in the district once known as Deadman's Place.

In the 17th Century a Mr Dyer, the licensee of a tavern here in **Deadman's Place (13)** (pp 39, 92), was much troubled by the ghost of his late wife. The unquiet spirit began with a bit of poltergeist activity but soon resorted to more theatrical attempts to attract his attention, appearing in ever-more terrifying guises. Once, when he fell to his knees to pray for deliverance, she whacked him with an old pot, leaving him paralysed in one arm. Driven from his haunted tavern, the luckless Dyer twice moved house: first to Rochester Yard, then to Winchester Yard, close to St Mary Overie's Stairs. The vengeful ghost followed him, disturbing his sleep with increasingly violent apparitions and one night almost strangling him in his bed. It is not recorded whether or not her ghost was eventually exorcised, or whether she carried her husband off to dwell with her in the land of shades.

Let us reflect soberly on Dyer's tale as we walk up the cobbled alley that is Clink Street – now scrubbed clean of valuable graffiti – its refurbished warehouses tastefully enhanced by the fake skeleton suspended in an iron cage above the Clink Prison Museum. Fifty metres up on the right is the skeleton of **Winchester Palace (14)** (pp 19, 39–40), with its Rose Window still intact. The ruin was only exposed in 1814, when the warehouse in which it had been bricked up was destroyed in a fire. Subsequent excavations revealed the remains of a 2nd-century Roman bath-house. The statue of a British hunter god,

SECRET BANKSIDE

found nearby in the foundations of the Cathedral, implied that the Roman complex included a temple. For reasons best known to English Heritage, the huge stone cross that had lain exposed in the foundations was covered up, encased in sand.

At the end of Clink Street, turn sharp left and walk up to **St Mary Overie dock (15)**. The dock is mentioned in the Domesday Book; its landing fees were divided between the King and the Bishop of Winchester. Tudor historian John Stow mentions 'a house of sisters, founded by a maiden named Mary' to which she bequeathed the 'oversight and profits of a cross ferry over the Thames'. 'Overie' is an archaic word meaning 'over the river'. A granite plaque by the dock relates one version of the Mary Overie legend. Here's my own variant of the tale:

Back in the Dark Ages, Mary Overie's father, John Overs, was a Thames ferryman. He obviously did pretty well for himself: he's said to have owned most of the land around here – but he was also a dreadful miser – so mean that he faked his own death in the hope that his grieving family and servants would fast out of respect and so save him the cost of feeding them.

But he can't resist sneaking back, to see how they're getting on with their mourning – only to find them having a party – glad to be rid of him! Worst of all, they've raided his wine-cellars and are helping themselves to his precious food stores. Old Man Overie bursts in upon them, forgetting that he's supposed to be dead. A quick-witted waterman, thinking it's a ghost 'or the Devil himself', grabs an oar and clubs him to death.

His daughter Mary inherited his wealth and estates. Her fiancé, making haste to marry her and claim her inheritance, fell from his horse, suffering fatal head injuries. It's said that, interpreting these two deaths as a sign from God, she founded a 7th-century Bankside convent on the site of a Roman temple. During the 9th Century the nuns were removed, supposedly to protect them from rampaging Danes and Norsemen. They were replaced by Augustinian 'black priors', though their priory continued to bear her name. It was rebuilt in 1106 and again after the great fire of 1212. During the 12th Century, the parish Church of St Mary Overie was built to minister to the needs of Bankside residents. It subsequently became known as St Saviour's (pp 21–2, 40–1), which in turn begot Southwark Cathedral.

Moored in the dock is The Golden Hinde, a working replica of Sir Francis Drake's ship, which has no historical link with the dock or Bankside – an instance of recent efforts to reinvent Bankside as 'Ye Olde Theme Parke'. Resisting its charms, we walk away from the dock, down Cathedral Street; then left, skirting the railings of Cathedral Yard; then right, under the railway arches through **Green Dragon Court (16)**. Austin Osman Spare considered renting here in 1947, but even the down-at-heel occultist seems to have been put off by the squalor – not to mention the din of the cathedral bells. Turn left down Bedale Street to come out on Borough High Street. Cross Borough High Street and walk down St Thomas Street.

On our left, the red-brick building with the tower is **The Old Operating Theatre and Herb Garret Museum (17)** – all that remains of the old St Thomas' Hospital (pp 118–9), which was forced out by the coming of the railway to London Bridge. The Operating Theatre was closed and sealed in 1862 and was only rediscovered in 1956. Its wooden floor-boards provide perfect sounding-boards for phantom footsteps. A photograph taken in the Herb Garret shows a spectral apparition; some have claimed it as the ghost of Florence Nightingale, who founded her nursing school at St Thomas' Hospital.

Carry on down St Thomas Street, past Guy's Hospital on our right, with the London Bridge railway arches on our left. Past Stainer Street, take the next left, Weston Street, a suitably spooky – not to say brimstone-stenched – tunnel under London Bridge. Walk up the tunnel towards Tooley Street. The skeleton of a horse was discovered bricked into the walls in the caverns on our left – the original site of **The Drome (18)** (pp 69–70), now SeOne club. I mentioned the horse skeleton on one of my public ghost walks. A walker interrupted to relate how he and a friend had been walking in this deserted neighbourhood one Sunday morning. They followed the sound of clopping hooves into the tunnel, but there was not a horse in sight!

More unexplained sounds – including sneezes and whistling – have often been reported in the arches housing the **Britain At War (19)** exhibition, on our right as we emerge into Tooley Street. We turn left, walking up to **The London Dungeon (20)**. In 1998, psychic investigators who spent the night here (allegedly) found it brimming with ghosts. They filmed spectral faces appearing from a brick wall and a skeleton that seemed spontaneously to grow new flesh. One researcher claimed to have been slapped in the face by a ghost. The report appears to be genuine, though any horror museum's claim to be haunted should perhaps be taken with a healthy dose of salt.

Walk on up Tooley Street, past The London Dungeon, to the Joiner Street entrance to London Bridge rail and underground stations. With the station entrance behind us, we cross the road and go straight on to St Olaf House. To the left of this elegant Art Deco office building, go through Olaf Stairs to the riverside walk. From here we can see the Thames from London Bridge (left) to Tower Bridge (right). If we hear ghostly cries emanating from **London Bridge (21)** (pp 42, 53–5), it may be the ghosts of drowned Jewish deportees. In 1290, the Jews were expelled by Edward I. The exiles had boarded a ship which got stranded on a sandbank near London Bridge. The captain told his passengers to wait on the sandbank for the tide to turn. However, as the water rose, he sailed away, leaving them to drown.

Or they could be the cries of older, Danish ghosts. In 1014 the Danes had occupied the bridge. The Norwegian King Olaf blithely sailed under it, attached ropes to the supports and rowed off downstream, demolishing the bridge and hurling the Danish army into the river. This spectacular reversal of fortune – and the

Detail of the old London Bridge from Wenceslaus Hollar, 'Long View of London' (1636–42)

saga celebrating it – is believed to be the origin of the nursery rhyme 'London Bridge is falling down'.

Or the yet more ancient voices of children. A ring-ditch, the remains of an earth barrow, was excavated at Fennings Wharf (now Number 1 London Bridge).[2] In it was found evidence of numerous cremations performed over a long period spanning the bronze and Iron Ages. Most of the human remains discovered here were of children.

Across the river, the **Church of St Magnus the Martyr (22)** is said to be haunted by the black-robed ghost of a former rector, Miles Coverdale, still searching for something in the vicinity of his tomb. It was Coverdale who commissioned the first English translation of the Bible, 'Imprinted in Southwark at St Thomas' Hospital by James Nicolson, 1537'.

To the east, on the far bank, looms the forbidding shape of **The Tower of London (23)**. The Tower is a ghost-hunter's paradise – though the resident spooks seem to be stuck in a hell of eternal recurrence. King Henry VI was (allegedly) murdered in the Wakefield Tower by the soon-to-be Richard III on the 21 May 1471. His ghost is said to appear there at midnight on the anniversary of his death. In 1483 Edward and Richard, the Princes in the Bloody Tower, were also (allegedly) murdered, on their Uncle Richard's orders. Their ghosts still return to haunt their prison cell, whimpering and shivering in their night-gowns.

According to Celtic legend, the decapitated head of the god Bran was buried over there in the Bryn Gwyn, or 'White Mound', where it remained for ages, defending England from invasion – until King Arthur rashly removed it, whereupon these isles fell prey to waves of invaders: Saxons, Danes, Normans... When William the Conqueror took London, he built his White Tower on the Bryn Gwyn, symbolically asserting his dominion over this land. It was in this very White Tower where, four centuries later, Catrin Glyndwr, daughter of the rebel Owain, and her children were imprisoned and died. It is said to be haunted by a mysterious Lady in White. Incidentally, the name Bran is Welsh for 'crow' – a possible connection with the ravens that guard the Tower.

Tower Green, the place of execution, is *the* place of recurring nightmares, haunted by those whose lives ended there, including Anne Boleyn, Lady Jane Grey and Margaret Pole, who defiantly refused to kneel: 'So should traitors do, and I am none.' The executioner chased her around the block and hacked her to pieces. They say her blood-curdling screams can still be heard on 27 May, the anniversary of her death.

We could go on – I personally like the one about the Beefeater guard who was almost throttled by a phantom strangler – but life's too short! Let's end this Ghost Walk by going one step beyond the hocus pocus…

In 1912 a Roman jug was unearthed on the Thames mud-flats close to where we're standing now. It bore the inscription: 'Londini Ad Fanum Isidis' ('In London at the Temple of Isis'). The cult of Isis, the Egyptian goddess, was brought to London by the Romans, who identified her with Venus. Her official temple was in The City on the north bank. However, antiquarians have cited the jug as evidence that her cult was operating in this vicinity in the 1st and 2nd Centuries. The legend of Isis and Osiris is itself an extraordinary tale of resurrection and return from the dead:

When Osiris was murdered by his jealous brother Seth, Isis retrieved his body. With the help of charms provided by the god Thoth, she managed to breathe some life into his corpse – enough, at least, to raise his manhood. She then fluttered above him in the form of a bird, enabling him to impregnate her, and so conceived their child Horus. Knowing that Seth would kill Horus, she fled into the marshlands of the Nile Delta, disguising herself as a beggar-woman. When Seth found Osiris' body, he chopped it into pieces and scattered them throughout Egypt, believing that this would prevent the god's resurrection. Isis wandered the land, carefully retrieving her dismembered husband's body-parts and putting him back together. Unable to find his penis, which had been swallowed by a fish, she fashioned him a replacement phallus. Then, helped by Thoth and Anubis, Horus bandaged and embalmed Osiris' body, using his own Eye of Horus to bring his father back from the dead. This myth is the probable origin of the Egyptian practices of mummification and the 'Opening of the Mouth' ritual. Horus, Isis, her sister Nephthys and Thoth then escorted Osiris on his ascent to heaven, where he was enthroned as Lord and Judge of The Dead.

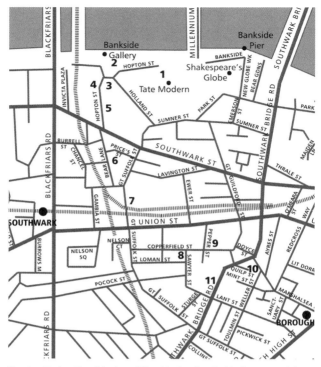

Route: *Facing* Tate Modern (**1**) *with the river behind us, turn right and walk upstream, with the river on our right, along Hopton Street to the junction with Holland Street. Here was the area formerly known as* Paris Garden (**2**)*, the location of* The Swan theatre (**3**) *and the brothel known as* Holland's Leaguer (**4**)*. Walk past the left-hand turning into Holland Street, taking the next left and following Hopton Street away from the river. On the left-hand side of the road are* Hopton's Alms Houses (**5**)*. Walk down Hopton Street to the junction with Southwark Street. Cross the road. Continue down* Bear Lane (**6**)*, and on down* Great Suffolk Street (**7**)*. Crossing Union Street, take the next left down Copperfield Street, passing* Winchester Cottages (**8**) *on the right and, on the left, at the far end of the street,* All Hallows Church and Gardens (**9**)*. Go across Great Guildford Street, and cut through Doyce Street to Southwark Bridge Road. Turn right and walk south. Across the road on the left is* Mint Street Park (**10**) *and, a little further down on the right, the* Fire Station (**11**)*.

Tate to Elephant

From Tate Modern art gallery, an international visitor attraction, to the Elephant and Castle, now in the process of 'regeneration', by way of a short-cut through the back-streets of what were once St George's Fields. Along the way we encounter time-honoured trades and industries, along with other curious facets of south London history.

Walk begins: *Tate Modern, the Jubilee Walkway by the river.*
  Ends: *The Elephant and Castle.*

Duration: *short, 30–60 minutes.*

Transport links – Start: *Southwark underground station. Bus: RV1.* **Finish:** *Elephant and Castle underground and rail stations.*

THIS WALK IS DEFINED more by its route than a specific theme or period of history. It is, quite simply, a pleasant short-cut from Tate Modern to the Elephant and Castle, through the back-streets of what were once St George's Fields. Along the way, we'll sample some of the subjects explored in more depth on the other walks. We'll incidentally be helping to deliver the much-heralded 'trickle-down' effect of 'regeneration', which is supposed to lure visitors and new wealth southwards – from Bankside's tourist attractions and prime river-front real estate down to the socially deprived Elephant.

Tate Modern (1) was created in the shell of the New Bankside Power station, an oil-fired 1950s power station on the south bank, facing St Paul's. Its architect was Sir Giles Gilbert Scott, who also designed Britain's red telephone box and Waterloo Bridge. More than 4 million bricks were used in the construction of the brick-clad steel structure, with its hundred-metre high central chimney. It stood empty from 1981 until 1994, when the Tate Gallery acquired an option on the site and set about its conversion. Tate Modern opened in 2000. Its galleries house a comprehensive modern art collection, though the New British Artists are under-represented, the early works of Damien Hirst & Co. having been snapped up by the Saatchi Collection.

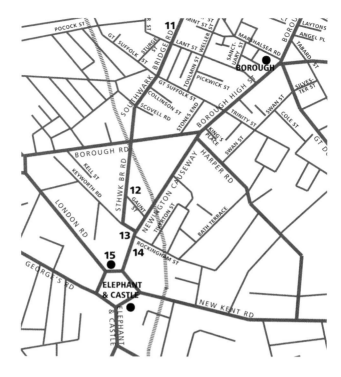

Route (cont.): *Go on down Southwark Bridge Road, across Borough Road, then turn left to walk along Gaunt Street, with* The Ministry of Sound (**12**) *on our left. At the bottom of Gaunt Street, turn right and go south down* Newington Causeway (**13**). *Across the road to our left is* Alexander Fleming House (**14**). *The* Elephant and Castle (**15**) *is at the end of Newington Causeway, with the Bakerloo Line Underground Station on the corner.*

Tate Modern's star exhibit is the building itself, the magnificent Turbine Hall providing the setting for some of its most ambitious and enormous artworks. Louise Bourgeois created giant spiders and spiral staircases ascending to platforms surrounded by mirrors – turning visitors into exhibits. Amish Kapoor filled the hall with a lurid, visceral red flower, while Rachel Whiteread created an entirely different effect with stacks of white boxes. Perhaps the most effective interactive artwork was Olafur Eliasson's *A Weather Project*. The south end of the Turbine Hall was dominated by a pale sun shining in an artificial mist; the ceiling was transformed into an enormous mirror. Groups of visitors would lie on the floor, using their bodies to spell out words – in reverse, so as to be legible when reflected. During a visit by US President George Bush, activists wrote anti-Bush slogans in block capitals on the ceiling with their bodies.

Walk upstream, with the river on our right, along Hopton Street to the junction with Holland Street. On the waterfront is Falcon Point, site of the once famous Falcon Inn. During the Middle Ages, this was part of **Paris Garden (2)**, another of the south bank's anomalous, semi-autonomous manors (pp 18–9). The land was previously owned by Cluniac monks. In 1313 King Edward II took over the 'mills of Widflete' ('willow stream') from the Knights Templar, along with a garden called the Paris Garden. The name may come from Robert de Paris, who owned the Manor House here in the 14th Century, or may derive from the French 'pareil' ('an enclosure'). It's still the name of a street just to the west of here, off Stamford Street. By Jacobean times Paris Garden Manor had effectively coalesced with the Clink Liberty to form the waterfront pleasure district known as Bankside.

The Swan theatre (3) (p 34) once stood here at the junction of Hopton Street and Holland Street (formerly 'The Green Walk' and 'Gravel Lane' respectively). Just to the west of here was The Manor House, home to the infamous stew later immortalised as **Holland's Leaguer (4)** (pp 19–21). In the 1632 novel of that name, the Madame, Dame Elizabeth Holland, also known as 'Dona Hollandia',

> was most taken with the report of three famous amphitheatres, which stood so near situated that her eye might take view of them from the lowest turret.

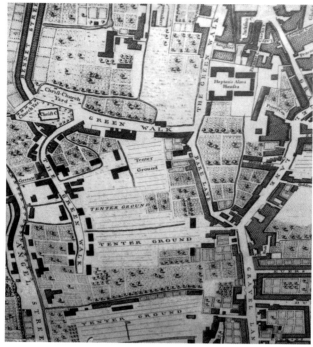

Rocque's map (1739–47), detail

Dame Elizabeth's interest was not purely aesthetic. The 'beauties and brave spirits' who packed the theatres also provided her own clientele. During the winter of 1631–2 her stew, which was surrounded by a moat, was besieged by troops. The Dutch working girls put up a spirited defence, raising the drawbridge and pelting the troops with ordure.

Walk past Holland Street on the left, then take the next left, following Hopton Street away from the river. This street is named after Charles Hopton, who died in 1730, and whose endowment provided for the building of 26 almshouses. **Hopton's Alms Houses (5)** are marked on John Rocque's map of 1739–47, on what is called 'The Green Walk'. According to Hopton's Alms Houses' book of rules, tenants could be fined for swearing, 'resorting to alehouses' and for 'railing, bitter or uncharitable speech'. These dignified Georgian almshouses can still be seen here on the left-hand side of Hopton Street.

SECRET BANKSIDE

Walk on down Hopton Street to the junction with Southwark Street. About 50 metres away to the left, just off Sumner Street, is Falcon Close, the site of the Baptist Zoar Chapel, where the author of *The Pilgrim's Progress,* John Bunyan, is supposed to have preached. It was obliterated during a Second World War bombing raid. The Zoar Chapel was one of a number of Nonconformist chapels and meeting-houses in the area, testifying to south London's proud tradition of Protestant dissent. Just to the west was a Unitarian Church on Stamford Street; to the south, Rowland Hill's Surrey Chapel on Blackfriars Road (p 65) and the Welsh Congregational Chapel on Southwark Bridge Road; to the east, an Independent meeting-house at Deadman's Place and a Quaker meeting-house in Redcross Way. 'Zoar', as in the nearby Zoar Street, is the biblical name for a sanctuary.

In 1790 the Pott brothers opened a large vinegar works in the vicinity. Theirs predated the more famous Sarson's Vinegar works, a couple of kilometres to the east in Bermondsey, which survived well into the 20th Century. Like Bermondsey, this area would have been steeped in the sweet smell of vinegar, mingled with less appetising odours.

Crossing Southwark Street, carry on straight down **Bear Lane (6)**, whose name recalls the local bear-pits of yore. The cruel 'sport' was established as a Bankside entertainment by the mid-16th Century (pp 34–5). Bears were baited for the amusement of King Henry VIII during his 1539 visit to Paris Garden. The King took the sensible precaution of watching from the safety of his royal barge; in the event, a bear broke free and boarded one of the other boats, causing it to overturn. Many bears became local celebrities: one called Harry Hunks even had a poem written about him. It didn't save him from being blinded to provide a new diversion: 'whipping the blind bear'. Thomas Dekker witnessed his torments:

> a blind bear was tied to the stake, and instead of baiting him with dogs, a company of creatures that had the shapes of men and faces of Christians (being either colliers, carters or watermen) took the office of beadles upon them, and whipped Monsieur Hunks till the blood ran down his old shoulders.

At the next junction, bear right and continue south down **Great Suffolk Street (7)**. The street was developed in the late 18th Century, assimilating part of Gravel Lane. It extended southwards over Dirty Lane, then a muddy track through the marshes. The street was renamed after Suffolk Palace, the London home of Charles Brandon, Duke of Suffolk. The palace stood across the road from the Church of St George the Martyr. A royal mint operated there. It lent its name to The Mint (pp 27, 49–50), the outlaws' sanctuary to the east – on our left as we walk down Great Suffolk Street.

As late as the 18th Century this area, then known as St George's Fields, was open marshland, part of the Lambeth Marsh that stretched east as far as Deptford. The marsh was criss-crossed by footpaths with names like Dirty Lane and Bandyleg Walk. The first Christ Church was erected in 1671 on what is now Blackfriars Road. Within fifty years it was sinking into the mud. It was rebuilt, on firmer foundations, in 1741. The present church was built in 1960.

Crossing Union Street, take the next left down Copperfield Street. **Winchester Cottages (8)**, the row of terraced cottages on the right, were built in the 1890s, an example of the social housing and other charitable projects which proliferated in this area. Such philanthropic traditions go back at least to the 16th Century, when Thomas Cure established his almshouses in Deadman's Place. In Victorian times, the American philanthropist George Peabody endowed the creation of Peabody Estates providing affordable housing for working people, whilst Octavia Hill oversaw the creation of Red Cross Cottages (pp 27–8, 121) and estates off the Walworth Road (p 107). The roads between Waterloo and The Borough are graced with a large number of hostels, missions and campaigning organisations.

At the far end of Copperfield Street, on the left, is the shell of **All Hallows Church (9)** framing a garden of contemplation. The original church, built in 1880, was destroyed during the Second World War. Its successor now houses a recording studio. The gothic arch, the ivy-clad wall backing the gardens, and the wooden cross with its stark image of the crucified Christ – all testify to what was here before.

Copperfield Street leads into the south end of Great Guildford Street, which takes its name from the county town of Surrey. On the left, a few metres up the street, St Mungo's Hostel continues to provide shelter for rough sleepers. We continue

Sign at rear of Borough Welsh Congregational Chapel, Doyce Street

more or less straight on, cutting through Doyce Street to Southwark Bridge Road, past the stern notice at the back of the Borough Welsh Congregational Chapel: 'Commit No Nuisance'.

Across the road is **Mint Street Park (10)**, former site of the Mint Street Workhouse (p 47) and the Evelina Hospital 'for sick children' (p 121): some original gratings can still be seen, set into the wall. Turn right and walk south down Southwark Bridge Road, where Thomas Bowler invented the famous 'bowler hat'. In the mid-19th Century, there were more than 3000 hatters working in this area. By then, the many local crafts workshops and warehouses were being crowded out by smoke-belching factories. One commentator wrote:

> Southwark is as distinguishable by its tall chimneys and clouds of smoke emitted by them, as is London for its church spires.

A little further down on the right is the **New Central Fire Brigade Station (11)**. 'New' in 1878, it was extended in 1883 and again in 1910. The complex includes a training school and Winchester House – the former residence of Captain Eyre Massey Shaw, first chief of the Metropolitan Fire Brigade. Known as 'Skipper' to his men, whom he recruited from the ranks of former sailors, the Captain's prowess – as a fireman and as a ladies' man – is immortalised in Gilbert and Sullivan's *Iolanthe:*

> Oh, Captain Shaw!
> Type of true love kept under!

> Could thy brigade, with cold cascade
> Quench my great love, I wonder?

The station still houses The Borough's fire engines. Just off Marshalsea Road, now behind us on the far side of Mint Street Park, is Ayres Street, commemorating Alice Ayres, a children's nurse who died in 1885 in a fire on Union Street, sacrificing her own life to save three children in her care.

Go on down Southwark Bridge Road, across Borough Road, then left into Gaunt Street. On our left, **The Ministry of Sound (12)** is arguably the most famous dance club in the world. The Ministry's glory days may be gone – by the late 1990s the scene had moved on to clubs like The Drome (pp 69–70) – but the weekend queues still snake out around Newington Causeway.

At the end of Gaunt Street, look left to admire the psychedelic lighting on the railway bridge, then turn right into **Newington Causeway (13)**. The Romans built the original causeway to carry Stane Street over the marshes. A map of 1681 shows a maypole erected here. By Victorian times the Newington Tollgate tithed all traffic using the causeway.

In 1921, Dr Cecil Belfield Clarke, born in Barbados, opened his GP's surgery at 112 Newington Causeway, going on to serve this community for more than 40 years. In 1931, together with Dr Harold Moody, who had his practice in Peckham, Dr Clarke helped found the League of Coloured Peoples to campaign for the rights of African and Caribbean settlers.

Over the road is **Alexander Fleming House (14)**, a listed building. Its former DSS offices have been refurbished to create the residential apartments of Metro Heights.

At the south end of Newington Causeway is **The Elephant and Castle (15)**, a long-established transport hub. In 1641, back in the days of horse-drawn carriages, blacksmith John Flaxman set up his forge on an island between the roads. In the 18th Century, the smithy became The White Horse inn, later renamed The Elephant and Castle. An elephant with a castle on its back was the sign of the Cutler's Company, perhaps because of the ivory used on cutlery handles. There is seemingly no truth in the popular belief that the name is a corruption of the 'Infanta de Castile'.

Turnpike Trusts, established in the mid-18th Century, oversaw the upkeep of stretches of road and the building of new roads. One such trust was responsible for building the New Kent Road, which bears off to our left. In 1862, the railway came to challenge Thomas Tilling's four-horse omnibus. Dickens (pp 45–55) evokes the changing times in this place of

> little shops lying somewhere in that ganglion of roads from Kent and Surrey and of streets from the bridges of London, centring in the far-famed Elephant who has lost his Castle formed of a thousand four-horse coaches, to a stronger iron monster than he, ready to chop him up into mincemeat any day he dares. (*Bleak House*)

The railway line that Dickens is referring to crosses Newington Causeway and New Kent Road on viaducts, those Victorian brick arches which have long since been colonised by workshops and warehouses – and more recently by clubs and parties.

The 'tube' opened in 1890. The Northern Line was the first electric railway in a deep underground tunnel – more than fifteen metres deep at the Elephant. 1906 saw the opening of the Baker Street and Waterloo ('Bakerloo') Line.

The Elephant was devastated during the Blitz of 1941, although it's generally agreed that post-war planners did more damage than the German Luftwaffe. Ever since its redevelopment in the 1960s, the Elephant and Castle's vast gyratory traffic system has forced pedestrians underground into a labyrinth of grimy subways. The subways are being phased out and the traffic re-routed around a huge plaza, as part of the Elephant's ongoing transformation. One hopes that the people behind the current regeneration project will have learned the lessons of the past – that communities cannot be designed and delivered from on high – and that new developments will take account of the needs of local people.

And here we are: Elephant and Castle, with the original Bakerloo line tube station round the corner on our right, and stops for buses to all parts of south-east London conveniently situated nearby.

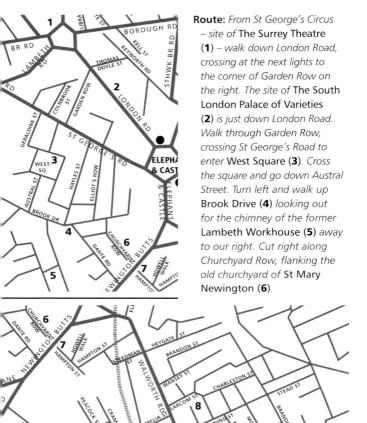

Route: *From St George's Circus – site of* **The Surrey Theatre** (**1**) *– walk down London Road, crossing at the next lights to the corner of Garden Row on the right. The site of* **The South London Palace of Varieties** (**2**) *is just down London Road. Walk through Garden Row, crossing St George's Road to enter* **West Square** (**3**). *Cross the square and go down Austral Street. Turn left and walk up* **Brook Drive** (**4**) *looking out for the chimney of the former* **Lambeth Workhouse** (**5**) *away to our right. Cut right along Churchyard Row, flanking the old churchyard of* **St Mary Newington** (**6**).

Cross **Newington Butts** (**7**), *go down Hampton Street, bearing left to come out on the Walworth Road. Turn right, heading south down Walworth Road. Take the third turning on the left, Larcom Street, walking up to* **St John's Church** (**8**). *Cut through the alley on the right, past the church, turn left along Charleston Street, then right down Brandon Street, to the junction with* **East Street** (**9**). *Continue straight across East Street down Portland Street. Turn right down Liverpool Grove and go in through the side gate on the right to* **St Peter's Church** (**10**).

Charlie Chaplin's Memory Lane

How 'The Little Tramp' was born of the Elephant and Castle. This walk traces Chaplin's childhood on the streets of south London. With most common land taken over by factories and tenement housing, the Victorian working-class resorted to taverns and public pleasure gardens, 'penny-gaff' theatres and music halls like the South London Palace of Varieties.

Walk begins: *St George's Circus, corner of Borough Road and London Road. This walk loops down around the Walworth Road and back to the Elephant.* **Ends:** *Elephant and Castle.*

Duration: *long, 90–120 minutes.*

Transport links – Start: *Elephant and Castle, Lambeth North or Southwark underground station (roughly equidistant, 5–10 minutes walk).* **Finish:** *Elephant and Castle underground and rail stations.*

SOUTH LONDON'S CELEBRATED MUSIC HALLS were all dotted around Lambeth Marsh. A kilometre west of here, on Lower Marsh, close to what is now Waterloo, was The Canterbury Arms – 'the mother of music hall'. Astley's Amphitheatre opened in 1769, presenting its circus and variety acts for more than a century on a site near Westminster Bridge. Its first proprietor Philip Astley performed equestrian feats and a 'Hercules' strongman act – hence Hercules Road, North Lambeth, named after Hercules Buildings, Astley's terrace where William Blake (pp 129–31) and his wife rented a house in the 1790s. On the other side of the marsh, a couple of kilometres east of here, was The Star in Abbey Street, Bermondsey.

Like the Bankside theatres in Shakespeare's day (p 31), such establishments were blamed for all the ills of society. The Rotunda, a penny-gaff just up Blackfriars Road, was condemned as 'a den of juvenile crime and delinquency'. The Duke's Head on Redcross Way was 'a moral-corrupting meeting house'. In that

Route (cont.): *Go across the back of* St Peter's Church (**10**)*, turn left and walk through the Monkey Park garden. Go out of the front gate, doubling back in through the gate immediately beside it. Walk through the churchyard, keeping the church on our left to complete our circle around it, then go back out the side gate through which we first entered. Cross Liverpool Grove, cut through Lytham Street, opposite, and turn right into* Merrow Street (**11**)*. Cross Walworth Road and walk down Fielding Street. Follow the road round as it turns into Penrose Street. Walk along to the* Beehive pub (**12**)*, then turn left and walk down Carter Street to face St Paul's Church. Turn right and walk along Chapter Road, then go in through the gates on the right to Pasley Park, formerly part of* Surrey Gardens (**13**) *and site of the* Surrey Gardens Theatre (**14**)*.*

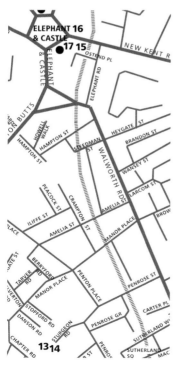

Bear left, keeping the railings on our left, to cross Pasley Park, coming out on Manor Place. Turn right and walk east down Manor Place to the junction, then turn left onto Walworth Road and walk up towards the Elephant and Castle. Turn right and walk up Elephant Road, with the railway viaduct on our left, onto the New Kent Road. Turn left and walk under the railway bridge to The Coronet, site of The Elephant and Castle Theatre (**15**)*. The Trocadero (**16**) stood on the other side of the New Kent Road. Next door to The Coronet is* The Charlie Chaplin pub (**17**)*.*

same disreputable neighbourhood, on Great Suffolk Street, less than a kilometre north-east of here, were The Borough Music Hall (aka The Salmon and, from 1879, The Raglan) and The Surrey Music Hall, later known as The Winchester tavern.

We begin here, at St George's Circus, where an 18th-century obelisk marks the distances to Westminster and The City. According to Dickens,

> Those that are acquainted with London are aware of a locality on the Surrey side of the Thames called the Obelisk, or more generally, the Obstacle.

We're standing on the east side, on the corner of Borough Road and London Road. To the north-west, on the far side of the obelisk, in the 'V' of land formed by the junction of Waterloo Road and Blackfriars Road, is the former site of **The Surrey Theatre (1)**. It opened in 1782 as The Royal Circus and Equestrian Philharmonic Academy, inspired by Astley's Amphitheatre which had been packing them in for more than a decade. It went bust. It burnt down. It got rebuilt. In 1809 it passed into the hands of the actor-manager Robert Elliston. He hit on the idea of featuring a ballet in every play he staged, even Shakespearean tragedies, so as to get round the Patent Act under which only certain licensed theatres could produce plays. During most of its life, The Surrey staged popular melodramas. The Black American actor Ira Aldridge raised the tone, playing Othello here in 1833 and again in

'A View of the Royal Circus in St George's Fields' from *The Westminster Magazine*, 30 September 1782. The Surrey Theatre is on the right. The obelisk can just be seen in the far left of the picture.

1848. Unauthorised dramatisations of Charles Dickens' novels *Oliver Twist* and *Nicholas Nickleby* were also presented, to popular acclaim. According to his biographer John Forster,

> one version at the Royal Surrey Theatre was so excruciatingly bad that in the middle of the first scene the agonised novelist lay down on the floor of his box and never rose until the curtain fell.

The novelist's anguish may have been caused by the realisation that he would earn no royalties from the pirated adaptation.

From 1881 until 1901, The Surrey Theatre was run by George Conquest, an aerialist who claimed to have perfected the art of stage 'flying' and, in the process, to have broken every bone in his body! In 1920 it was converted into a cinema, and was demolished in 1934 to make way for an extension of the Royal Ophthalmic Hospital. A student hall of residence now occupies the site.

From St George's Circus, we walk down London Road, crossing at the next lights to stand on the corner of Garden Row. Further down the road we can see the South Bank University buildings on the former site of The South London Palace of Varieties, close to the Bakerloo Line tube station. Bombed during the Blitz, this famous music hall was demolished in 1955. We could walk down and take a closer look, but of the old music hall there's really nothing left to see.

The South London Palace of Varieties (2) (aka The South London Music Hall, aka 'The Sarf') had opened in 1860. With a capacity of 4000, it was *the* great south London music hall. Variety stars like Marie Lloyd and Dan Leno performed here, along with performing dogs, skipping-rope dancers, acrobats and illusionists – not forgetting 'Lollo, Lillo and Otto, the bicycle wonders of the age'. The eclectic assortment of variety acts were kept in some sort of order by its bantering 'Chairman', Baron Courteney, famous for his oversized diamond cuff-links, studs and rings – the 19th-century equivalent of 'bling'.

Charlie Chaplin performed at the South London Palace of Varieties as a member of Fred Karno's Company. His mother Hannah had appeared here, under her stage name Lily Harley. Her name is on the playbill for Thursday 27 May 1886, though

'The "South London" in 1870 – London's First Palace of Varieties'
from *The South London Palace Journal no. 1*

she receives no byline and is listed well below 'Vesta Tilley, London Idol'. The male impersonator Vesta Tilley was one of the highest-paid vaudevillians of the decade.

At the bottom of the same bill we find Marie Lloyd, then aged only 16. The following year she got pregnant by a 'stage-door Johnny' named Percy Courtenay and had to get married – her sister Alice called it a 'walking wedding'. It didn't last, and Marie would go on to marry twice more. By 1891 she was topping the bill in music halls throughout the land. She moved her extended family into a mansion in New Cross, a couple of kilometres east of here. Though she toured widely, Marie often returned to The South London Palace. By the dawn of the 20th Century she was an internationally famous, if controversial, star. Many of her best-loved songs – such as 'A Little Of What You Fancy Does You Good' – featured *double entendres*, which she pointed up in performance with winks and knowing looks, though it was generally agreed that she was 'suggestive but never vulgar'. The poet T S Eliot was moved to write of her death as 'a significant moment in English history'.

Go along Garden Row, past the site of a Lactarium that once dispensed milk and syllabubs to 18th-century visitors, and across St George's Road to enter West Square, built around an attractive public garden.

In his *Autobiography* Charlie Chaplin remembers his time in **West Square (3)** with affection, but his happy childhood was short-lived. His father deserted the family. By the time Charlie was five, in 1894, his mother Hannah's health, and singing voice, were failing. Her stage career had stalled, and her estranged husband was refusing to support them. She and the children would go on to live at more than fifty addresses in the area, often 'doing a runner' in the middle of the night, and sometimes winding up in the workhouse. A sign on a wall in nearby Geraldine Street reminds us that West Square stood in the shadow of Bethlem (or 'Bedlam') psychiatric hospital. Mental illness would cast its own long shadow over Hannah's later life. The square bears no trace of their stay here; the plaque in the right-hand corner honours J A R Newlands, the chemist who discovered the Periodic Law.

To find a plaque to Chaplin we'd have to walk all the way down to Number 287 Kennington Road, where Charlie and his brother Sidney lodged with their father and his lover, a woman called Louise. Charles Senior was an alcoholic who died of cirrhosis of the liver in 1901, aged 37. This probably wasn't helped by the fact that Charlie's Uncle Spencer was landlord of The Queen's Head pub in nearby Black Prince Road. After his father's death Charlie, wearing a black armband to garner sympathy, earned money selling flowers in local pubs. His mother made him stop his lucrative scam.

Again in his *Autobiography,* Chaplin links his stage debut – in Aldershot, aged five – with his mother Hannah's last professional appearance. Her voice cracked in the middle of a song. The crowd started jeering, and she left the stage, a broken woman. Charlie came to her rescue, coming on to sing a song called 'Jack Jones'. The delighted audience showered the stage with coins. Charlie stopped – mid-performance – to pick them up, causing great hilarity, especially when the stage manager tried to help him. Thinking that the man intended to keep the change, Charlie anxiously followed him off-stage, to gales of laughter. Hannah and Charlie were living at Pownall (or Parnell) Terrace, also down Kennington Road, when he returned home one day to be told that his mother had gone insane. She'd been handing out lumps of coal to the street urchins as 'birthday presents'. Hannah was sent to an asylum where she received electric shock treatment.

On the far side of West Square, go down Austral Street to **Brook Drive (4)**, home, in her later life, to the pioneering African-American variety artist Connie Smith. She and her husband Gus worked the south London music halls, playing piano duets and helping to popularise the cake-walk dance. After Gus's death, Connie found work as an actress. In 1956, aged 80, she played Tituba in *The Crucible* at the Royal Court. On her death in 1970, a mass was read for her in St George's Cathedral.[1]

Turn left and walk up Brook Drive. A little further along, away to the right, we can glimpse the grim brick chimney from the old **Lambeth Workhouse (5)** where the Chaplin boys and their mother were housed for a time. Workhouse registers show that, in the years 1896–8, Charles and his brother Sidney were also in the Hanwell Schools 'for orphans and destitute children' about 12 miles away.

From Brook Drive we cut right along Churchyard Row, flanking the old churchyard of **St Mary Newington (6)**. The land is said to have been granted by the Saxon King Edmund to his jester Hitard, the first in a long line of local 'fools' or clowns, whose 19th-century music hall heyday culminated spectacularly in 'The Little Tramp' himself. Chaplin's celebrated clown character was almost certainly inspired by the desperate men who inhabited his own south London neighbourhood. He's said to have based his walk on an old man who fed the horses at the Elephant and Castle.

Cross **Newington Butts (7)** where, in 1576, Peter Hunningbourne built an Elizabethan playhouse, pre-dating Bankside's Rose and Globe theatres by more than a decade. Go down Hampton Street, bearing left to come out on the Walworth Road. Turn right, heading south down Walworth Road. Numbers 144 to 152 in the Georgian terrace on the right were the former headquarters of the Labour Party. Across the road is an impressive group of red-brick buildings. The first, the Vestry Hall of St Mary Newington Parish, later Southwark Town Hall, now houses the Cuming Museum, an eclectic collection of antiquities and curiosities collected by Richard Cuming and his son, and bequeathed to the Borough of Southwark in 1902. Beside it is Newington Library and a third building, once the Health Services Department, whose outer wall still bears the inscription: 'The

Health Of The People Is The Highest Law'. During the 19th Century, the parish of St Mary Newington saw a huge population increase: in 1801, it was less than 15,000; 80 years later it was over 100,000.

Turn left down Larcom Street. Thirty metres along on the right is **St John's Church (8)** where, in the late 19th Century, the Reverend Arthur Jephson conducted 'penny marriages' for the poor. Here, on 22 June 1885, Hannah Harriet Hill married Charles Chaplin Senior. The address on their marriage certificate is given as 57 Brandon Street. Hannah (aka Lily) was already the single mother of Sidney, whom she claimed was the son of a lord with whom she'd run off to Africa. The 1891 census shows the Chaplin family living at 94 Barlow Street, Walworth.

Cut through the alley by the church and follow Charleston Street along to the junction; then turn right and walk down Brandon Street to the crossing with **East Street (9)**, one of south London's most famous street markets, celebrated in the coster-songs of Victorian Music Hall. Coster-mongers were fruit'n'veg men – the word may derive from 'custard-apple'. Prior to 1871, their stalls used to spill out onto the Walworth Road. The coming of the trams pushed them back into East Street. Stall-holders would gather at dawn in the surrounding streets, ready to fight for a decent pitch. In 1927, the system of issuing Borough Council licences was introduced in an attempt to restore harmony – or at least order! Back then, East Street was popularly known as 'The Lane'.

Chaplin's grandfather, Charles Hill, an Irish cobbler, supposedly had a shop in East Street; he and Charlie's grandmother both ended up in the workhouse. Charlie claimed to have been born 'on April 16th 1889' in 'East Lane'. However, there is no official record of his birth – and he was hardly a reliable witness to his own life, often changing his stories to suit his 'rags to riches' legend. Even his date of birth is uncertain. According to an announcement in the *The Cradle* (11 May 1889), 'on the 15th ultimo, the wife of Mr Charles Chaplin (née Miss Lily Harley) of a beautiful boy. Mother and son both doing well'.

Carry on across East Street, where Brandon Street turns into Portland Street. Another fifty metres or so down Portland Street, the more recent utilitarian social housing gives way to a pleasant, early 20th-century estate. Turn right down Liverpool Grove and go in – through the side gate in the railings on the right – to **St Peter's Church (10)**, built by the designer of the Bank of England, Sir John Soane, in 1825. The congregation was initially segregated on class lines: the well-to-do paid for their pews; their servants and other working people sat upstairs, with galleries beside the organ pipes for the 'Charity Children'. Around 1895, the Reverend John Horsley began providing free meals for poor children in the crypt. In the rectory garden, he started a zoo, known locally as the Monkey Park.

Go around the back of the church to where the gravestones have been stacked, their shapes echoed by the graffiti on the brick wall behind them. Turn left and walk through the Monkey Park garden, with the church on our left and with the Inspire Café and community centre in its crypt. During both World Wars, people sheltered from bombs in the crypt. In 1940 two bombs hit the church, killing 65 people and injuring many more. The night-club scenes in the controversial BBC series *The Singing Detective* were filmed here.

Come out of St Peter's front gate, doubling back in through the gate immediately beside it. Walk through the churchyard, keeping the church on our left to complete our circle around it, then go back out the side gate through which we first entered. Cross Liverpool Grove, cut through Lytham Street, opposite, and turn right into **Merrow Street (11)** where, in 1904, Octavia Hill oversaw the building of an estate for the poor people of Walworth. This entire area has been designated the Octavia Hill Conservation Area.

Crossing the Walworth Road, we walk down Fielding Street. In 1800, Walworth was a small, elegant and relatively affluent suburb, surrounded by open country. Within a century the commons had been enclosed and developed, crammed with tenements, craft workshops and factories. The surviving allotments to our right give a sense of the old rural Walworth.

On the left-hand side of Fielding Street is Pelier Park, with Pelier Street beyond, the site of the original Montpelier Tavern

'The Music Hall, Surrey Zoological Gardens'

and Tea Gardens. The Montpelier Palace, a rudimentary music hall, opened in the back of the tavern in 1853. In 1891 it burnt down – and was promptly rebuilt, reopening under a succession of names: The Montpelier, The Empire Music Hall, then The Walworth Empire. The final curtain fell in 1919.

Follow Fielding Street round as it turns into Penrose Street. Walk along to the corner of Penrose and Carter Street. Across the road on the right is the **Beehive pub (12)**. It used to look out onto the Beehive Tea Gardens, where people sat in wooden arbours around an expanse of green. The Montpelier Cricket Club was formed here, and played on the Beehive ground from around 1840. The cricketers later moved on to the Oval, re-forming as Surrey County Cricket Club. Only this attractive period pub remains.

Turn left into Carter Street and walk down to face St Paul's Church in Lorrimore Square. Turn right into Chapter Road and walk up beside the park railings on the right. Go in through the gate to Pasley Park – all that's left of the old Lorrimore Common. From 1831 until 1878 all this was part of **Surrey Gardens (13)**, an 'attractive pleasure grounds adorned with statuary and fountains and a magnificent lake'. The lake was used as the foreground for the staging of epic panoramas with fireworks, such as Vesuvius erupting across the Bay of Naples.

In the collection of the Cuming Museum, which we passed earlier on Walworth Road, are posters and a handbill from 1837 for the Royal Surrey Zoological Gardens advertising 'Mrs Graham's Balloon Ascents – the only female aeronaut in Europe'.

The zoo, itself only part of the whole Surrey Gardens experience, attracted thousands of visitors each day. Queen Victoria paid a royal visit; she was intrigued to see a dog and a tiger amicably sharing a cage. Along with the usual big beasts of the jungle, Surrey Gardens also boasted a giant tortoise and the first giraffes to be seen in an English zoo, brought from Africa by an Arab called Fadlallah.

In 1856 the zoo closed, but **The Surrey Gardens Theatre (14)**, also dating from 1831, survived, seating up to 10,000 people. In 1857, a charity concert was held there, in aid of the Jamaican nurse Mary Seacole's work in the Crimea. Seacole had established The British Hotel near Balaclava, providing nurses and creature comforts for the troops. When she returned to England, bankrupt, *Punch* magazine published a song, 'Dame Sea Cole', encouraging its readers to support her work. The Seacole Fund was launched, culminating in a fund-raising concert in The Surrey Gardens Theatre – a kind of 19th-century 'Band Aid'. The French conductor Louis Jullien's 300-strong orchestra was supplemented by 11 military bands, the Royal Italian Opera Company and the Royal Surrey Choral Society, a total of nearly 1000 performers! Mary Seacole was guest of honour. At the end of the concert, *The Times* reported that

> the genial old lady rose from her place and smiled benignantly on the assembled multitude, amid a tremendous and continued cheering.[2]

To cross Pasley Park, bear left and walk roughly fifty metres north to come out on Manor Place – facing Walworth Garden Farm, which provides horticultural training for local people. Turn right and walk east down Manor Place. On the right are the former Manor Place public baths, dating from 1898, when the local tenement houses had no bathrooms of their own. The building reopened in 2007 as the Samye Dzong Tibetan Buddhist Centre. Go down to the junction, turn left onto Walworth Road and walk up towards the Elephant and Castle.

Just before the railway bridge, we take the right turn and walk up Elephant Road, with the railway viaduct on our left, onto the New Kent Road. Less than a kilometre away to our right, up by the Bricklayer's Arms, it turns into the *Old* Kent Road, immortalised in Albert Chevalier's music-hall hit 'Knocked 'Em In the Old Kent Road'.

We, however, turn left, back along the *New* Kent Road. Just the other side of the railway bridge, The Coronet night-club stands on the site of **The Elephant and Castle Theatre (15)** which opened in 1872, staging melodramas. In 1928 it was converted into the ABC cinema (later renamed The Coronet) with a capacity of over 2000 and a Wurlitzer organ that rose up from the pit.

Just across the road was **The Trocadero (16)**. Some old-timers can still remember the night in 1937 when the famous black actor, singer and activist Paul Robeson got up on stage at 'The Troc' and performed a selection of hit songs, including 'Old Man River', before a screening of *King Solomon's Mines*. Robeson's co-star in the film *Song of Freedom*, the black singer Belle Davis, also sang in local music halls including The South London Palace of Varieties.[3]

And what became of Charlie Chaplin, the boy from the Elephant? In his teens he performed as a Jewish comedian under the name Sam Cohen. His brother Sidney had joined Fred Karno's Company and persuaded Karno to give Charlie a job. The story goes that Charlie, then aged 17, had to borrow a pair of shoes which were much too big for him. The big shoes became his trademark. Also in the troupe was Arthur Stanley Jefferson, who would later become famous as Stan Laurel. They performed in many south London music halls, including The Peckham Hippodrome and The South London Palace.

In 1910, Charlie Chaplin went with the Karno Company to the United States. In 1913, aged 24, he signed for the US film production company Keystone for $150 per week. Six years later, he founded United Artists with D W Griffith, Mary Pickford and Douglas Fairbanks. Chaplin's silent films include *The Tramp*, *The Kid* and *The Gold Rush*; his sound movies include *City Lights*, *Modern Times* and *The Great Dictator*. Films like *Easy Street* were undoubtedly influenced by memories of his deprived childhood.

In later life, on a visit to London, the by then world-famous Hollywood star stayed at The Savoy Hotel in a room with a view over the river to the south bank. He also revisited his childhood haunts around the Elephant, reputedly drinking a martini in the pub that still stands next door to The Coronet. We may care to follow his example, and to raise our glass to 'The Little Tramp' in the bar of **The Charlie Chaplin (17)**.

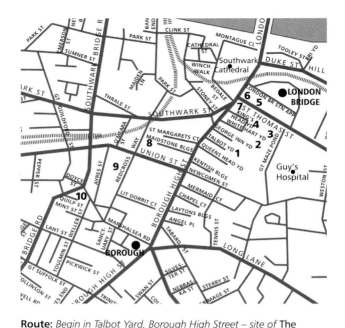

Route: *Begin in Talbot Yard, Borough High Street – site of* The Tabard (**1**). *Walk through the yard, past Guy's mortuary, turning left through the arch, then follow the lane round into the grounds of* Guy's Hospital (**2**). *Go up the steps on the left and through the Guy's House colonnade, passing the* Lunatick Chair (**3**) *in the quadrangle on the right. Walk through the front courtyard, visiting* Guy's Chapel (**4**) *on the left. Coming out of the chapel, go left out of the courtyard. Turn left and walk up St Thomas Street. On our right is The Old Operating Theatre and Herb Garret Museum on the former site of* St Thomas' Hospital (**5**) *and, at what is now* Number 1 St Thomas Street (**6**) *– between the church and the High Street – the site of a 2nd-century pit complex containing dog sacrifices. On our left, a plaque at* Number 8 St Thomas Street (**7**) *records that John Keats briefly lodged here. At the end of St Thomas Street, turn left down Borough High Street, crossing at the lights to take the right fork along Southwark Street, then left down Redcross Way to the shrine at the gates of* Cross Bones Graveyard (**8**). *Continue down Redcross Way past* Red Cross Garden (**9**) *on our right. At the end of Redcross Way, cross Marshalsea Road and turn right, then take the park entrance on the left to cut through* Mint Street Park (**10**).

A Healing Pilgrimage

This walk takes Chaucer's Canterbury Tales, *which begin in Southwark, as the starting point for a walk about 'healing' in an urban environment: from Guy's and the original St Thomas' Hospital to the former Bedlam, taking in the sites of old prisons and burial grounds which have since been reclaimed as public parks and gardens.*

Walk begins: *Talbot Yard, Borough High Street.* **Ends:** *The Peace Garden, Imperial War Museum.*

Duration: *medium, 60–90 minutes.*

Transport links – Start: *London Bridge underground and rail stations.* **Finish:** *Lambeth North, Southwark or Elephant and Castle underground stations (roughly equidistant, 5–10 minutes walk).*

TALBOT YARD TAKES ITS NAME from The Talbot, the pub that stood here until its demolition. 'Talbot' (a breed of hunting dog) may have been a corruption of 'Tabard' ('a medieval tunic'), the original name of the inn that stood here back in the late 14th Century – when London Bridge was the only bridge over the Thames, and the gateway to Canterbury; **The Tabard (1)** was the original Pilgrims' Inn – as in Chaucer's *Canterbury Tales*:

> In Southwark at the Tabard as I lay
> Ready to set off on my pilgrimage

In Geoffrey Chaucer's day, if you suffered from sickness or infirmity, or even if you didn't, you'd go on pilgrimage to a sacred site, to ask for a healing miracle or simply to give thanks for your health. And the most sacred site in England was the tomb of St Thomas à Becket.

Becket had been friend and counsellor to the young Henry II – medieval urban myth has them cementing their friendship in the Bankside brothels. Archdeacon Thomas Becket was signatory to the Royal Ordinances of 1161 'touching the

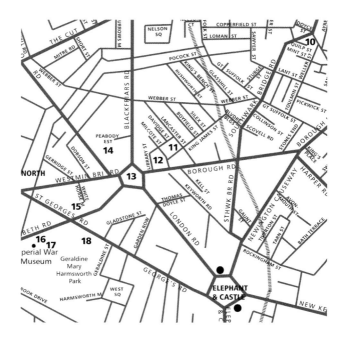

Route (cont.): *Walk out onto Southwark Bridge Road, turn left, walking down past Sawyer Street. At the next junction, turn right, and then take the left fork down Webber Street. Just before the railway bridge, we turn left and walk down Belvedere Buildings, then right under the viaduct into King James Street. At the far end of King James Street is the* **BOST Diversity Garden** **(11)**. *Turn left to join Borough Road, where we turn right and walk up past the former* **Passmore Edwards Public Library** **(12)**. *Walk up to* **St George's Circus** **(13)**. *Just north of here was the* **Magdalen Hospital** **(14)**. *At the roundabout, take the second left down Lambeth Road.* **St George's Roman Catholic Cathedral** **(15)** *stands on the north side of Lambeth Road, facing across the junction towards the site of the former* **St Mary of Bethlem Hospital** **(16)**, *now the* **Imperial War Museum** **(17)**. *In the grounds of the Museum – also known as Geraldine Mary Harmsworth Park – is the* **Tibetan Peace Garden** **(18)**.

government of the Stewholders in Southwark under the direction of the Bishop of Winchester' (pp 19–20). He went on to become Archbishop of Canterbury – and be murdered, on the King's orders, in his own cathedral. Within ten years of his death, his shrine had reportedly been the scene – and the presumed cause – of some 700 miracles.

Miracles. The blind see. Lepers and other 'incurables' are inexplicably healed. The medieval Lock Hospital for lepers – the 'lazar house' – stood by St Thomas à Watering, the stream where Chaucer's pilgrims stop to pray on the road to Canterbury. It's now the Bricklayer's Arms with its huge roundabout and flyover at the confluence of the Old and New Kent Roads, a kilometre south of here.

The Canterbury Tales is framed by a sacred pilgrimage, yet Chaucer's spiritual vision is revealed in the profane tales the pilgrims tell along the way. His is a warts-and-all portrayal of humanity – the coarse Miller, the noble Knight, the lusty wife of Bath may have been based on actual travellers he met here at The Tabard. We know that landlord Harry Bailly was a real person, the MP for Southwark and licensee of The Tabard. He it is who suggests that the pilgrims tell each other stories, who promises to reward the teller of the best tale with a slap-up meal on the house. Harry Bailly, purveyor of sustenance to poets – arguably the true father of English literature!

Walk on down Talbot Yard past Guy's Mortuary, then left under the arch into **Guy's Hospital (2)**. Thomas Guy was a Bermondsey boy, born around 1645 on Fair Street,

'The Talbot Inn, 1828' – formerly The Tabard

Horselydown. Having established himself as a bookseller and printer, he endowed wards in St Thomas' Hospital, of which he was a governor. Guy made his fortune by investing in the South Sea Company, selling off his inflated stock shortly before the 'bubble' burst. He determined to use his windfall to found the hospital that still bears his name. With the help of Queen Anne's physician Richard Mead he established a hospital for those who 'may be adjudged or called Incurable and as such not proper Objects to be received into [...] the present Hospital of St Thomas'. The original Guy's House, with its colonnade and quadrangles was completed by 1726. Extensions, including the east wing with the chapel, were progressively added over the next half century.

Follow the lane round towards Guy's Tower. The newer buildings over to the right are part of King's College. Go up the steps on the left and through the Guy's House colonnade. The black and white mosaic paving was added during restoration work in 1899. In the quadrangle to the right is a stone alcove known as the **Lunatick Chair (3)**. It was one of fourteen alcoves salvaged from the 1831 demolition of London Bridge (p 55). The hospital bought it for ten guineas, installing it in the wall of the 'Lunatick House' from which it takes its name.

Walk through to where the bronze statue of Thomas Guy dominates the front courtyard. Step inside **Guy's Chapel (4)**

'The Lunatick Chair', Guy's Hospital

to view the founder's marble memorial: 'He provided a Retreat for hopeless Insanity and rivalled the endowments of Kings'. A plaque on the wall facing the outer door commemorates Astley Cooper: 'The Undisputed [...] First Surgeon of his Age'. In 1789, aged 21, he became Demonstrator of Anatomy at Guy's, where he subsequently established a medical school.

For centuries, medical knowledge had been hampered by religious taboos against dissecting corpses, influenced by the Christian belief in the resurrection of the body. The body-snatchers who provided the corpses used in anatomy classes were known ironically as 'Resurrectionists'. The surgeons helped subsidise

The Old Operating Theatre and Herb Garret Museum

their work, bribing the authorities to keep them out of prison and supporting their families when they were doing time. Astley Cooper himself was obliged to do business with the Borough Boys, a local gang led by former prize-fighter Ben Crouch. The Burke and Hare scandal in Edinburgh hastened the passing of the Anatomy Act, which allowed unclaimed corpses from workhouses to be used for medical research. However, the controversy over the use of human remains continues to this day.

During the 1990s, the threat of closure provoked an energetic 'Save Guy's' campaign. Guy's was duly saved. The opening of a King's College campus in its grounds will hopefully help secure the hospital's survival for the foreseeable future.

Walk out of the courtyard, turning left into St Thomas Street. Across the road is St Thomas' Church, with its imposing brick tower now housing The Old Operating Theatre and Herb Garret Museum, all that remains of the old **St Thomas' Hospital (5)**. St Thomas' cult was established long before Chaucer's pilgrims set off for Canterbury. The hospital dedicated to him was rebuilt on this site when the fire of 1212 destroyed the original hospital in the Priory of St Mary Overie. In 1223 the Bishop of Winchester, Peter de Rupibus, made an annual endowment to 'the ancient hospital built of old to entertain the poor'.

The hospital soon acquired a reputation to match the neighbourhood it served. In 1535, Thomas Cromwell spoke of 'the bawdy hospital of St Thomas in Southwark'. The following year Edith Percke was charged with operating a brothel inside the hospital. It was shut down in 1540, but reopened just over a decade later by Royal Decree: 'in view of the sick and infirm poor men lying begging in the public streets […] to the infection and annoyance of the King's subjects'. With the cult of St Thomas the Martyr having been suppressed during the Reformation, the dedication was subtly reassigned to St Thomas the Apostle.

Back in the 15th Century, Lord Mayor Dick Whittington had endowed a ward for 'young women that had done amiss', but from 1561 the hospital refused to treat unmarried pregnant women, rejecting them as 'harlots'. In Victorian times the hospital maintained separate 'foul' wards – imaginatively named 'Lazarus', 'Job' and 'Magdalen' – for patients suffering from venereal diseases.

One pioneering surgeon, William Cheselden, joined the hospital in 1718. He made his reputation as a lithotomist, claiming he could remove a gallstone in less than a minute. Cheselden wore a silk turban (instead of a wig) during surgery, thereby significantly reducing the risk of infection. In 1745 he founded the Company of Surgeons (as distinct from Barber-Surgeons), the forerunner of the Royal College of Surgeons.

By 1703 Thomas Cartwright, master mason to Christopher Wren, had finished rebuilding the medieval St Thomas' Church. In 1821 an operating theatre was constructed in the church tower, but in 1859 the entire site was acquired for the development of London Bridge Station. The hospital was temporarily rehoused in Surrey Gardens Zoo (pp 108–9), before moving to its present site by Westminster Bridge. The church became the Chapter House of Southwark Cathedral. The Old Operating Theatre was sealed up in the attic and forgotten for almost a century. Rediscovered in 1956, it is now part of the museum (p 69).

Excavations conducted prior to building work at what is now **Number 1 St Thomas Street (6)** – between the church and the High Street, once the south wing of the old hospital – uncovered a 2nd-century complex of wells and pits, containing what appear to be sacrificial offerings, including the skeletons of some twenty dogs. To the Celts, dogs symbolised death, healing and rebirth. They are associated with the river goddess Nantosuelta, whose totemic animals are dogs and ravens. This stretch of the Thames has yielded evidence of prehistoric offerings to river deities. The river goddess Nehalennia, often depicted with a dog and a raven, has been identified with Elen, whom some have proposed as the goddess of London who was later assimilated by Christians as St Helen.[1]

To recap: the hospital is originally part of the priory of St Mary Overie, Mary the ferryman's daughter (p 83), an apocryphal saint perhaps originating in a pagan river goddess; the hospital is subsequently rebuilt on the site of a pit containing what appear to be ritual offerings to a river deity. A Roman jug, found in the river mud a hundred metres from here, offers circumstantial evidence of a local Temple of Isis, goddess of healing and sexual love (p 87); the antiquarian E J Burford suggests that the prostitutes who serviced the Roman garrison in Southwark would have been initiates of her cult. This hospital is dedicated to St Thomas à Becket, who signed the ordinances legalising prostitution within the Liberty; the same hospital is subsequently accused of operating a brothel in one of its wards. Can all this be mere coincidence?

Across the road, a plaque at **Number 8 St Thomas Street (7)** records that

> On this site the poet and apothecary John Keats and his friend the poet apothecary surgeon & chemist Henry Stephens shared lodgings while studying at Guy's and St Thomas' Hospitals (1815–16).

Keats studied with Astley Cooper, and in 1816 was appointed dresser to the eminent surgeon William Lucas. (Not to be confused with his son, 'Billy the Butcher', whose patients suffered an alarmingly high mortality rate!) Between attending lectures and working as a dresser, Keats found time for writing poetry, boxing and sleeping with prostitutes, one of whom gave him a dose of the clap. Also in 1816, he had his first poem published – 'O Solitude!'. That summer, he moved to new lodgings in Dean Street (now under the railway in Stainer Street) where he wrote 'On First Looking Into Chapman's Homer'.

At the end of St Thomas Street, turn left down Borough High Street, crossing at the lights to take the right fork along Southwark Street, then left down Redcross Way to the shrine at the gates of Cross Bones, the unconsecrated burial ground for prostitutes and paupers.

Back in the 1990s **Cross Bones Graveyard (8)** (pp 28–9, 79–81) was a desolate place. By the Museum of London's own estimate, the site contained roughly 15,000 burials. Rumours abounded – that the archaeologists had had too little time to properly remove the human remains; that they'd been pushed out to make way for the Jubilee Line tunnellers – the locals told horror-tales of bones getting mashed in ancient charnel pits.

Since then, local people have created this shrine at the gates in Redcross Way. The names on the ribbons tied to the bars are apparently among the few names of people buried in Cross Bones that were recorded, during the century or so that records were even kept[*]. Even then, such names were entered under the generality of 'St Saviour's Churchyard'. However, from the entries in the register, it's possible to deduce who ended up with the prostitutes in this paupers' yard:

> March 10th 1727 – Ann Howard out of Our Poor […]
> gratis.
> July 24th 1833 – Mary Davis, Dead House.
> 18th September 1839 – Eliza Ann Solomon, Union Street,
> 1 month.
> December 21st 1728 – Morgan a female infant.
> 28th October 1840 – Margaret Donavon, Union
> Workhouse, 1 year.

With such names, it seems, people honour all the nameless, the forgotten souls:

> A Woman Out of The Street – October 31st 1726

Here too are hung amulets, crystals, feathers, shaman's beads; images of Christ, the Virgin, Buddha, pagan goddesses; tin skeletons (strictly Mexican day-of-the-dead); a knitted St George's

---

[*] The names of the dead inscribed on these ribbons are said to have been retrieved from St Saviour's burial registers in the London Metropolitan Archives.

cross; a totem you squeeze to make two tin cans clack together. This has every appearance of being an inclusive shrine, open to people of all faiths – and of none – a place to converse with the past, to remember, to reconnect.

With the co-operation of the present leaseholders, people meet regularly to clean and tend the wild garden in the oldest part of the site (to our right, as we look in through the gates). Having so far seen off various attempts to develop the site, locals are campaigning for this, the heart of Cross Bones, to be protected as a memorial garden. At a time when The Borough's open spaces are threatened by new developments, such a garden will be a powerful expression of healing in the inner city.

The exemplar for such a garden can be found a little further down the road, beyond the crossroads with Union Street. **Red Cross Garden (9)** is the legacy of Octavia Hill, the Victorian social reformer who campaigned for an 'open air sitting-room' to transform the lives of the underclass. Following its opening in 1887, she wrote: 'Nature smiles in darkest Southwark' (pp 27–8). By the late 20th Century the garden had fallen into neglect; it has recently been beautifully restored – complete with fountain and pool, though without its original bandstand. All over The Borough, once-sinister places have been reclaimed and greened: the exercise yard of Marshalsea Prison was turned into St George's Gardens; Horsemonger Lane Prison became Newington (or 'Jail') Gardens.

At the end of Redcross Way, cross Marshalsea Road and turn right, then take the park entrance on the left to cut through **Mint Street Park (10)**. Bankside Open Spaces Trust (BOST), which oversaw the restoration of Red Cross Garden, co-ordinates community gardening projects here at Mint Street and in other local parks and gardens. There are plans to create 'The Mint', a community centre with improved facilities, on what is now Mint Street Adventure Playground. The emphasis on providing a healthy, creative environment for young people is especially appropriate in a green open space that was once the site of both the Mint Street Workhouse (p 47) and then, later, the Evelina Hospital 'for sick children'. The hospital opened here in 1869, the gift of Baron de Rothschild in memory of his wife Evelina who had died giving birth. The Evelina Hospital survives to this day. In the 1970s it moved to Guy's Tower, and now occupies its own purpose-built, child-friendly building at St Thomas' Hospital, near Westminster Bridge.

Walk out onto Southwark Bridge Road, turn left, walking down past the fire station (pp 95–6) and across Sawyer Street. At the next junction, go right, then take the left fork down Webber Street. Just before the railway bridge, we turn left and walk down Belvedere Buildings, then go right under the viaduct into King James Street. We're passing through one of the last remnants of the old Victorian Borough, largely unchanged since the coming of the railways.

At the far end of King James Street is the BOST **Diversity Garden (11)**. Local people have grown vegetables, herbs and flowers in these community gardens.

Turn left to join Borough Road, where we turn right and walk up to the **Passmore Edwards Public Library (12)**, which opened in 1898. The introduction of public lending libraries was a vital aspect of Victorian efforts to raise the literacy and thus the living standards of the urban poor.

Walk on up to **St George's Circus (13)** with its 18th-century obelisk marking the distances to Westminster and the City. To the north of the roundabout stood The Surrey Theatre (pp 101–2). It was demolished in 1934 to make way for an

The Imperial War Museum, formerly St Mary of Bethlem Hospital

extension to the Royal Ophthalmic Hospital. A student hall of residence now stands on the site.

Just north of here was **Magdalen Hospital (14)** 'for the reception and training of penitent prostitutes', founded in 1758. The hospital was supported by collections made at public services held in the chapel. These were well attended – partly, no doubt, because they provided an opportunity to view the young 'Magdalens', who were obliged to attend services. In 1868 the hospital moved to Streatham. The site was sold to the Peabody Trust, who used it to build one of their first charitable housing estates – Peabody Square in Blackfriars Road.

Aside from her more obvious association with prostitution, Mary Magdalen was also identified as the woman out of whom Christ drove seven devils, an event interpreted by some as him healing her of a psychiatric disorder. Magdalen (or Maudlin) Hospitals also functioned as female psychiatric institutions. On John Cary's map of St George's Fields in 1787, a 'Magdalen Coffee House' stands just across the road from the hospital.

At the Circus, take the second left down Lambeth Road. During the 18th Century, South London pride in a fiercely independent Protestant tradition often spilled over into bigotry. The Irish Catholics who drained this marshland suffered discrimination and harassment. In 1780, a protest against the Catholic Relief Act rapidly degenerated into the Gordon Riots. The opening of **St George's Roman Catholic Cathedral (15)** in 1848 established a spiritual home for Southwark Catholics. Around that time, Father Thomas Doyle ministered mainly to the descendants of Irish and Italian immigrants; today its congregation also includes Nigerians, Colombians, Tamils, Mauritians and Poles. The Cathedral stands on the north side of Lambeth Road, facing across the junction towards the Imperial War Museum.

Around 1700, this area, known as St George's Fields, was open country. From the mid-18th Century a number of hospitals and charitable foundations established themselves here, no doubt in the belief that the country air would do their charges good. (In the event, the late 18th Century population explosion meant that the fields were soon built over, and the air quality declined accordingly.) The Philanthropic Society founded a reform school on a site now occupied by Notre Dame High School, on the corner of Lambeth Road and St George's Road. In 1799 a School for the Indigent Blind opened at The Dog and Duck tavern across the road in the grounds of what is now the Imperial War Museum.

The Dog and Duck – a tavern set amidst three ponds – had a spa of questionable purity, a bowling green and a swimming pool. In 1774, John Burgoyne parodied its pastoral charms:

> St George's Fields, with taste and fashion struck
> Display Arcadia at the Dog and Duck [...]
> To frowsy bowers they reel through midnight damps
> With Fawns half drunk, and Dryads breaking lamps.

We cross St George's Road to the Imperial War Museum, with two enormous guns guarding the entrance. Before it was a museum, it was 'Bedlam' – a corruption of 'Bethlem', as in the **St Mary of Bethlem Hospital (16)**. The famous psychiatric hospital occupied these buildings from 1815 until 1930, when it relocated to Monks Orchard in Kent. The hospital was formerly located over in The City – at Bishopsgate (1247–1676) and Moorfields (1676–1815).

For the character of Poor Mad Tom in *King Lear,* Shakespeare drew freely on the Bedlamite ballads sung by the poor unfortunates who wandered the land begging for small change – a 16th-century precursor of 'Care in the Community'. Such ballads served to alert passers-by to the singer's parlous state, yet they also developed their own heightened poetic forms, touchingly relating the doomed love of Mad Maud for Tom o' Bedlam:

> For to find my Tom o' Bedlam,
> Ten Thousand Years I'll Travel.
> Mad Maudlin goes with dirty toes
> For to save her boots from gravel.[2]

Mad Tom and Mad Maud can be seen as personifications of the male (Bethlem or 'Bedlam') and female (Magdalen or 'Maudlin') asylums. Mad Tom has his own phantasmagorical imagery:

> From the hag and hungry goblin
> That into rags would rend ye,

The spirit that stands by the naked man
In The Book of Moons defend thee.

His song celebrates a love that endures beyond the grave:

And I will find bonny Maud, merry Mad Maud,
And seek what e'er betides her,
And I will love beneath or above
The dirty earth that hides her.

The architect of this building – its imposing portico boasts six Ionic columns and a Coade stone crest – was Sidney Smirke, who also designed the original British Library's reading room dome. The copper dome was added in 1835, completing its chimerical appearance. Famous inmates included the painter Jonathan Martin, committed in 1829 for attempting to burn down York Minster; Edward Oxford, 1840, for trying to assassinate Queen Victoria; and the unfortunately named Richard Dadd, 1844, for attempting to kill his father. In a curious echo of the Old Man Overie story (p 83), Dadd claimed that he had believed his father to be the Devil in disguise. An accomplished painter, Dadd precisely delineated the sinister fairy worlds of his imagination.

In Georgian times, inmates were treated as objects of curiosity. Members of polite society paid to come and view them like objects in a freak-show. Their treatment was harsh to the point of cruelty, some of it verging on what we would now regard as torture. Here at Bethlem in the mid-19th Century Dr Charles Hood and George Henry Haydon pioneered a more compassionate approach. Wards were brightened and cheered with paintings, flowers and singing birds in cages. Patients were encouraged to read or listen to music. There were tea-parties and social events. Doctors and staff formed the Dog and Duck Club, named after the disreputable tavern that had stood on the site. Their amateur dramatic company performed comedies once a fortnight: a programme from 1879 shows them got up in turbans and blackface as characters from *Ali Baba*. (What *must* the patients have thought!) Haydon and Hood deserve to be counted among the Victorian fathers of psychotherapy.

Following the relocation of the hospital to Monks Orchard, the site was endowed by Viscount Rothermere to the people of Southwark – as a public park in memory of his mother Geraldine Mary Harmsworth. The wings of the hospital were demolished; in 1936 the main building, with its imposing green dome, became the **Imperial War Museum (17)**. Over the years the museum has had to adapt to changing public perceptions – the glorification of Empire yielding to a more considered and complex representation of the realities of warfare past and present.

We're facing the museum, with the big guns to our right. Ahead of us, a chunk of the old Berlin Wall shouts: 'CHANGE YOUR LIFE'.

We go left, through the gate in the low fence on our left to the **Tibetan Peace Garden (18)**. In the summer of 1996,

Buddhist monks set up a Peace Camp here, using coloured sand to create an intricate mandala (a symmetrical representation of spiritual harmony). The completed sand mandala was then destroyed, as a symbol of impermanence. Three years later the park was graced with this marginally more permanent Peace Garden. At the entrance a pillar bears a message from the Dalai Lama in Tibetan, English, Hindi and Chinese:

May this Peace Garden [...] remind us that human survival depends on living in harmony & on always choosing the path of non-violence in resolving our differences.

His Holiness came in person to consecrate the garden on 13 May 1999. There's an inner circle framed by four sculptures in white Portland stone – Air, Fire, Earth

Fragment of the Berlin Wall in the grounds of the Imperial War Museum

and Water – with a bronze Kalachakra mandala at its heart. What better place to sit and catch our breath – or focus on it! This is a place open to all, day and night – a place to meditate, to ask for help, or simply to express the heart's desire:

May all beings be free from suffering.

Route: *If coming from the Peace Garden, we go out of the front gates of the Imperial War museum, turn left and walk down Lambeth Road with the park on our left. At the next junction, turn right up Kennington Road, cross the road and take the first left along Cosser Street. Turn right at the junction to walk up Hercules Road. On our right is the Corporation of London's William Blake Estate, built on the site of* **Hercules Buildings (1)** *and near to all the sites on this walk:* **The Apollo Gardens (2)**, **The Flora Tea Gardens (3)**, **The Temple of Flora (4)** *and* **The Lambeth Asylum (5)**. *All these former landmarks have vanished, leaving virtually no trace. To revisit Blake's Lambeth requires a leap of imagination worthy of the visionary poet himself.*

Jerusalem Revisited

THIS IS NOT SO MUCH A WALK, more a short excursion, a pilgrimage to Blake's house in Lambeth. The former site of the house is marked by a plaque on the William Blake Estate, Hercules Road, just across the road from Lambeth North underground station.

The visit may be made as an optional extension of 'A Healing Pilgrimage'. If coming from the Peace Garden, we go out of the front gates of the Imperial War museum, turn left and walk down Lambeth Road with the park on our left. At the next junction, turn right up Kennington Road, cross the road and take the first left along Cosser Street. Turn right at the junction to walk up Hercules Road. On our right is the Corporation of London's William Blake Estate, built on the site of **Hercules Buildings (1)**. Half-way along the block there's a plaque on the wall:

> William Blake, poet & painter, lived in a house formerly on this site, 1793

We're here to honour the spirit of the man who once asserted: 'The road of excess leads to the palace of wisdom' (incidentally proving that the road of heightened perception doesn't necessarily lead to Bedlam!).

South London had been the cradle of William Blake's mystical visions: as a boy he'd seen a tree filled with angels at Peckham Rye. He returned in his thirties with his wife Catherine; they lived at Hercules Buildings from around 1791 until 1800. This was one of Blake's most prolific periods; he wrote *Songs of Innocence and Experience, The Marriage of Heaven and Hell* and other early 'Prophetic Books'. He self-published, experimenting with engraving techniques to illuminate his visions of eternity.

Yet during that single decade, as the population increased tenfold, Blake saw fields bricked over, new factories spewing chlorine, 'dark Satanic Mills' encroaching on his 'lovely Lambeth'. The original Albion Mills had opened in 1786 on Blackfriars Road, hailed as the first automated steam-driven flour mill. Barely five years later it had burnt down, amid rumours of arson. In Blake's poetic imagination its fire-blackened ruin became the embodiment of the mechanistic world-view against which he raged.

As common land dwindled, seedy fly-by-night pleasure gardens opened in his neighbourhood. They took their names from the classical gods: The Apollo Gardens, The Flora Tea Gardens, The Temple of Flora – none lasted even the decade:

> Beginning at Jerusalems Inner Court, Lambeth ruin'd and given
> To the detestable Gods of Priam, to Apollo: and at the Asylum
> Given to Hercules, who labour in Tirzahs Looms for bread.

The Apollo Gardens (2) were situated on what is now Pearman Street, to the north-east of Hercules Buildings. **The Flora Tea Gardens (3)** were just over the road from the Blakes, on what is now the corner of Hercules Road and Westminster Bridge Road. **The Temple of Flora (4)** was thirty metres north, close to the present-day junction of Baylis Road with Westminster Bridge Road; in 1796 it was shut down and its proprietor was thrown in the King's Bench for 'keeping a disorderly house'.

The **Lambeth Asylum for Girls (5)** stood just over the road from Hercules Buildings, in the triangle formed by Kennington Road and Westminster Bridge Road, on land now occupied by Christ Church. Founded in 1758 to provide a refuge for orphaned girls, it effectively operated as a workhouse. The girls were trained for domestic service or else condemned to menial work, such as that on offer in the mills.

> And was Jerusalem builded here
> Among these dark Satanic Mills?

Even as he wrestles with the darkness, Blake transforms it, investing it with new meanings in his eternal drama. The material world in general and Lambeth in all its 'Minute Particulars' are revealed as expressions of spiritual states:

There is a Grain of Sand in Lambeth that Satan cannot
    find
Nor can his Watch Fiends find it; 'tis translucent and has
    many Angles,
But he who finds it will find Oothoon's palace; for within
Opening into Beulah, every angle is a lovely heaven.
But should the watch Fiends find it, they would call it sin.

It was at their house in Hercules Buildings that Thomas
Butts once came upon Blake and his wife naked in their garden,
reciting Milton's *Paradise Lost*. Blake was reportedly not in the
least perturbed: 'Come in! It's only Adam and Eve, you know!'

Notes

The Ghost Walk

1 I am grateful to Christopher Jones for his research into Austin Osman Spare's various addresses around Walworth and The Borough. In his radical pamphlet *Nine Things That Aren't There* – itself a microcosmic masterpiece of psycho-geography – Jones identifies the Elephant and Castle roundabout as: 'The locus, the omphalos, the centrifugal heart of the territory of Austin Osman Spare'. I am also obliged to him for retrieving the advertisement for Spare's 1949 Temple Bar exhibition.

2 Thanks to Neil Gordon-Orr for alerting me to the Fennings Wharf ring-ditch.

Charlie Chaplin's Memory Lane

1 Connie Smith's story, along with those of other pioneering black actors and entertainers, is lovingly reconstructed by Stephen Bourne in *Speak of me as I am: The Black presence in Southwark since 1600* (London, Southwark Local History Library, 2005), pp 42–5

2 Quoted in Bourne, *Speak of me as I am*, p 30

3 *ibid*, pp 53–61

A Healing Pilgrimage

1 I am indebted to Steve Ash and Neil Gordon-Orr for independently sharing with me their research into pagan river goddesses in relation to the dog burials in St Thomas Street.

2 'Loving Mad Tom', the definitive essay on the Bedlamite ballads, is published in *The Crowning Privilege – Collected Essays on Poetry* (Harmondsworth, Penguin Books, 1959) by Robert Graves.

Jerusalem Revisited

1 I am obliged to Peter Ackroyd for decoding the geographical references in the three lines quoted above – and specifically 'the Asylum / Given to Hercules'. See *Blake* (London, Sinclair-Stevenson, 1995) p 129.

Illustrations

Unless stated otherwise, all illustrations are reproduced by permission of Southwark Local Studies Library.

Frontispiece: detail from 'Long View of London' (1636–42) by Wenceslaus Hollar.

Page 19: 'Remains of the great Hall of Winchester House as they appeared in 1820' from *The Gentleman's Magazine*.

Page 20: 'A Common Whore' by Andrzej Klimowski, based on a 17th-century woodcut. Reproduced from *The Southwark Mysteries* (London, Oberon, 1999).

Page 34: 'The Bear Garden' (left) and 'The Globe Theatre' (right) 'Engraved for Encyclopedia Londoniensis 1825', based on an early 17th-century woodcut.

Page 47: 'Mint Street Workhouse'.

Page 49: 'Mint Street looking towards High Street' from *The Builder*, 5 November 1853.

Page 53: 'The Meeting' by George Cruikshank, from an early edition of Charles Dickens' *Oliver Twist* in the author's collection.

Page 78: 'The Death Posture: Second Position' from *Ethos* by Austin Osman Spare (Thame, I-H-O Books, c.2000). By permission of I-H-O Books.

Page 85: detail from 'Long View of London' (1636–42) by Wenceslaus Hollar.

Page 92: detail from John Rocques' map (1739–47).

Page 101: 'A View of the Royal Circus in St George's Fields' from *The Westminster Magazine*, 30 September 1782.

Page 103: 'The "South London" in 1870 – London's First Palace of Varieties' from *The South London Palace Journal no. 1*.

Page 108: 'The Music Hall, Surrey Zoological Gardens'.

Page 115 : The Talbot Inn, 1828'.

Acknowledgements & Bibliography

I would especially like to thank to Katie Nicholls, my agent Nicki Stoddart and my publisher James Hogan for believing in this little book of walks, and Will Hammond and Dan Steward for editing it.

My primary research was conducted 'on the hoof' – walking the streets, talking to local people, seeing what was there and looking for clues as to what had been before. Only then did I follow up my leads in books. My thanks are due to Stephen Humphrey and the staff of Southwark Local Studies Library for their help and advice. Among the many publications which informed these walks, the following were particularly helpful:

Peter Ackroyd, *Blake* (London, Sinclair-Stevenson, 1995)

Peter Ackroyd, *Dickens* (London, Sinclair-Stevenson, 1990)

Stephen Bourne, *Speak of me as I am: The Black presence in Southwark since 1600* (London, Southwark Local History Library, 2005)

Julian Bowsher, *The Rose Theatre: an archaeological discovery* (London, Museum of London, 1998)

J A Brooks, *Ghosts of London: The West End, south and west* (Norwich, Jarrold Colour, 1982)

E J Burford, *The Bishop's Brothels* (London, Robert Hale, 1993)

Martha Carlin, *Medieval Southwark* (London, Hambledon Press, 1996)

Charlie Chaplin, *My Autobiography* (London, Bodley Head, 1964)

John Constable, *The Southwark Mysteries* (London, Oberon Books, 1999)

Barry Day, *This Wooden 'O': Shakespeare's Globe Reborn* (London, Oberon Books, 1996)

Charles Dickens, *Dickens' London: an imaginative vision* introduced by Peter Ackroyd, text by Piers Dudgeon (London, Headline, 1987)

Christopher Edwards (ed), *The London Theatre Guide 1576–1642* (London, The Bear Gardens Museum and Arts Centre, 1979)

Graham Gibberd, *On Lambeth Marsh: the South Bank and Waterloo* (London, J Gibberd, 1992)

Midge Gillies, *Marie Lloyd: The One and Only* (London, Gollancz, 1999)

Stephen Greenblatt, *Will in the World: How Shakespeare Became Shakespeare* (London, Jonathan Cape, 2004)

Shirley Harrison and Sally Evemy, *Southwark – Who Was Who: A Walk through Time with the Noble and the Nefarious* (London, London Borough of Southwark, 2001)

Christopher Hibbert, *The Making of Charles Dickens* (London, Longmans, 1967)

Stephen Humphrey, *An Introduction to the Cuming Family and the Cuming Museum* (London, Southwark Local Studies Library, 2002)

Christopher Jones, *Nine Things That Aren't There* (56a infoshop, London SE17 3AE)

Richard Jones, *Walking Haunted London* (London, New Holland, 1999)

William Kent (ed), *An Encyclopaedia of London* revised edition (London, J M Dent & Sons, 1951)

François Laroque, *Shakespeare: Court, Crowd and Playhouse* (London, Thames & Hudson, 1993)

Megan Brickley, *The Cross Bones burial ground, Redcross Way Southwark, London: archaeological excavations (1991–1998) for the London Underground Limited Jubilee Line Extension Project* MoLAS monograph 3 (London, Museum of Archaeology Service and Jubilee Line Extension Project, 1999)

Horace Monroe, *The Story of Southwark Cathedral* (London, Tuck & Sons, 1933)

Liza Picard, *Victorian London: the Life of a City 1840–1870* (London, Weidenfeld & Nicolson, 2005)

William Rendle, *Old Southwark and its People* (London, 1878)

Leonard Reilley and Geoff Marshall, *The Story of Bankside: from the River Thames to St George's Circus* (London, London Borough of Southwark, 2001)

Royal National Theatre Publications, *STAGEbySTAGE, The Development of the National Theatre 1848 to 1997*

Gāmini Salgādo, *The Elizabethan Underworld* (London, Dent, 1977)

Andrew Sanders, *Authors In Context: Charles Dickens* (Oxford, Oxford University Press, 2003)

James Shapiro, *1599: a year in the life of William Shakespeare* (London, Faber, 1995)

Southwark Public Libraries and Museums, *Charles Dickens and Southwark* (London, Council of the London Borough of Southwark, 1974)

John Stow, *A Survey of London: written in the year 1598* with an introduction by Antonia Fraser (Stroud, Sutton Publishing, 2005)

Richard Tames, *Southwark Past* (London, Historical Publications Ltd, 2001)

W Taylor, *Annals of St Mary Overie* (London, Nichols & Son, 1833)

See also:

www.southwark.gov.uk/DiscoverSouthwark/LocalStudiesLibrary

www.nationaltheatre.org.uk

www.into.org.uk/southwarkmysteries

www.gooseandcrow.co.uk

Index